HISTORY AS IT HAPPENED

MIDDLE EAST EXODUS

REFUGEE CRISIS IN EUROPE

The ☙INDEPENDENT

Mango Media
Miami
in collaboration with
The Independent

Independent Print Limited

Published by Mango Media, Inc.
www.mangomedia.us

This is a work of non-fiction adapted from articles and content by journalists of The Independent and published with permission.

Front Cover Image: Nicolas Economou/Shutterstock.com
Back Cover Image: gguy/Shutterstock.com

MIDDLE EAST EXODUS *Refugee Crisis in Europe*
ISBN: 978-1-63353-361-5

"If Europe fails on the question of refugees, then it won't be the Europe we wished for."

– Angela Merkel, German Chancellor

Table of Contents

PREFACE

The tragedy of the Middle East has brought about the greatest refugee migration since World War II and a crisis in Europe. Desperate people are pouring across borders in search of sanctuary or escape, and some believe the very existence of the EU could be at stake. The mood across Europe is hardening. Join us as journalists of the Independent explore this 21st century exodus.

PROLOGUE

SEEDS OF THE CRISIS

Syrian refugees at the Syria-Turkey border, 11 June 2011

19 October 2012
A TRICKLE OF SYRIAN ASYLUM SEEKERS BEFORE THE WAR

The number of Syrians claiming asylum in Britain has soared since civil war gripped the country last year.

Barely 10 a month sought refuge in the UK before President Bashar al-Assad's regime started turning its weaponry on protesters. The trickle has now turned into a stream of about 100 a month, placing fresh pressure on refugee support services and forcing the Home Office to issue new guidance to immigration officers dealing with Syrian asylum-seekers.

Some Syrians currently working or studying in Britain on visas which are about to run out are claiming asylum, warning they face arrest if they return to their home country. Most Syrians who make the journey to western Europe are seeking refuge in Germany, Switzerland or Sweden, but a significant minority are reaching the UK.

In the three months before civil war erupted last April, just 31 claimed asylum in Britain.In the final three months of the year, the number had risen to 149 - equivalent to 50 a month.

More than 330 claimed refuge in the first six months of 2012 - 55 a month - and unpublished Home Office figures suggest the number exceeded 100 a month in July and August.

Many have headed to London, but others have also arrived in Oxford. Asylum Welcome, which works with refugees in the city, has just sent out an alert to supporters asking for emergency help to look after new arrivals from Syria. It said: "[We are] providing support to the recent influx of Syrian families waiting to claim asylum and be relocated. This has put massive pressure on our resources, particularly the food cupboard which provides food for destitute families."

The UK Border Agency (UKBA) has just issued new guidance to staff handling asylum applications by Syrians. It warns that the Syrian security agencies routinely extract confessions by torturing suspects and locking up their relatives and estimates there are up to 3,000 political prisoners, most of whom have never been tried, in the country. But the UKBA also says there is no general policy against the enforced return of Syrians to Syria.

The Home Office, recognising the deepening crisis in the country, has just announced a temporary relaxation of the visa rules for Syrians legally in Britain. It said they would be able to apply to extend their stay without having to return home first. The Immigration minister, Mark Harper, said the concessions would remain in force until March. He added: "The Government continues to monitor the situation in Syria closely in order to ensure our response is appropriate."

Judith Dennis, policy officer at the Refugee Council said: "It is not surprising asylum claims from Syria have increased, given the serious human rights abuses that are taking place, leaving people with no choice but to flee for their lives. It is important for people to make the link between the situation they read about in the news and the impact on our fellow human beings. If they are not able to remain safe in their own country, it is right the UK does all it can to provide protection to those who need it."

'When I was shot at, I knew I couldn't return' Hasan Abdalla, 57, is a teacher who lived in the Kurdish region of north-eastern Syria. He came to Britain last December and, aided by Freedom From Torture, he was granted asylum in April. I first had problems with the regime 20 years ago when I was a member of the Kurdish Popular Union Party. They imprisoned me for one-and-a-half years - they said I had been distributing leaflets, but it wasn't me. I was beaten and tortured. They tie your legs up and hit you until you are unconscious, strap your hands to electric chairs with a cable connected to a car battery and shock you. "When the Arab Spring started we travelled down to Damascus to start holding demonstrations. They shot at us - two from my group and three others were killed. That was when I knew I had to run away.

"When I realised it was impossible for me to go back, I went to Turkey and found some agents to prepare a fake passport. I preferred Britain because I can speak English.

"I went to the Home Office and they gave me an appointment to apply for asylum. My family are in Jordan now and I want them to come and join me. I'm looking for a job as a translator for Arabic and Kurdish, and I've got a contract to start running a teaching course in London.

Barely 10 a month sought asylum before the war. In July and August, that figure exceeded 100 a month in July and August. Many have headed to London, but others have also arrived in Oxford. Asylum Welcome, which works with refugees in the city, has just sent out an alert to supporters asking for emergency help to look after new arrivals from Syria. It said: "[We are] providing support to the recent influx of Syrian families waiting to claim asylum and be relocated. This has put massive pressure on our resources, particularly the food cupboard which provides food for destitute families." The UK Border Agency (UKBA) has just issued new guidance to staff handling asylum applications by Syrians. It warns that the Syrian security agencies routinely extract confessions by torturing suspects and locking up their relatives and estimates there are up to 3,000 political prisoners, most of whom have never been tried, in the country. But the UKBA also says there is no general policy against the enforced return of Syrians to Syria.

The Home Office, recognising the deepening crisis in the country, has just announced a temporary relaxation of the visa rules for Syrians legally in Britain. It said they would be able to apply to extend their stay without having to return home first. The Immigration minister, Mark Harper, said the concessions would remain in force until March. He added: "The Government continues to monitor the situation in Syria closely in order to ensure our response is appropriate." Judith Dennis, policy officer at the Refugee Council said: "It is not surprising asylum claims from Syria have increased, given the serious human rights abuses that are taking place, leaving people with no choice but to flee for their lives. It is important for people to make the link between the situation they read about in the news and the impact on our fellow human beings. If they are not able to remain safe in their own country, it is right the UK does all it can to provide protection to those who need it."

Nigel Morris and Rob Hastings

2013

THE CRISIS BUILDS

Syrians at detention center, Pastrogor, Bulgaria, 25 September 2013

12 September 2013
LET'S OPEN OUR BORDERS TO SYRIA'S REFUGEES

Azad Sino fled with his wife and two children from the Syrian city of Aleppo nearly two years ago, when the carnage of civil war arrived on his doorstep. Since then, his family has been surviving in one cramped room in a flat just south of Beirut, with his health deteriorating and his wife forced to sell her jewellery to survive.

Yesterday, they were given the chance to salvage their shattered lives. They joined 103 other Syrians on a chartered plane to Hanover, the first of 25 flights in an airlift taking 5,000 refugees to Germany, which has granted them temporary sanctuary. This symbolic move takes the tiniest sliver of pressure off Lebanon, where every fourth person is now a Syrian and sectarian divisions are spilling over from its larger neighbour.

Amid all the talk in Westminster and Washington of intervention, along with honeyed words about helping victims of "the century's great tragedy", this flight is a reminder that there is something concrete Western countries can do to help other than wringing hands or firing missiles. So why is Britain not also offering refuge to some of those families whose lives have been ripped apart by this war?

Azad Sino is just one of two million people driven from their country, with another four million displaced within its borders. Everyone has their own horror story: homes destroyed, friends and family killed, families torn apart. With 5,000 people fleeing Syria each day - half of them children - the dangers of conflagration grow daily as the region struggles to cope with the influx. In Egypt, people are turning on Syrian refugees with violence and abuse. In Jordan, there is barely concealed anger over rising rents and food prices. Iraq, with sectarian violence exploding again, has shut its borders.

Last year 988 Syrians applied for asylum here, the majority accepted as genuine refugees. Yet Britain is one of the world's wealthiest nations, despite the downturn, and we should set a moral example by offering resettlement for thousands of the more vulnerable families. We already have a strong Syrian community of perhaps 5,000 people in this country; we could take in four times that number without too much trouble. History shows many would go back to their homeland when peace returned.

Such numbers would make only a small impression on the swelling tide of human misery. But if Britain joined Germany in setting a lead, we would be in a position to demand that other rich nations follow. During the Balkan crisis, this country took in nearly 20,000 refugees as part of a major European and US response. Yet while Europe takes in nearly two million immigrants a year from outside its borders, it has left Turkey to cope with 10 times as many Syrian refugees as the rest of the continent combined.

We are witnessing a national tragedy for Syria, a regional disaster, and a global problem. Instead of cheap talk or cruise missiles, how about some action to show we really care about this crisis?

Britain is one of the world's wealthiest nations. We should set an example.

Ian Birrell

3 November 2013

SYRIA'S CRISIS HITS EU'S POOREST NATION

This is not the Europe that Bangeen imagined. Crammed in a disused carpentry school on the outskirts of Sofia, the 32-year-old Syrian Kurd has fashioned a tent from a white sheet and a tree branch. It is enough to grant his family some privacy from the dozens of people sleeping in the classroom, but it cannot guard against the smell that seeps in from the corridor. Syrian refugees work around the clock sweeping floors, scrubbing bathrooms and laundering clothes. Their efforts, however, are futile given the sheer numbers arriving.

Bangeen's children cannot avoid the filth and broken glass littering the floor. When their clothes are washed, they will hang to dry in a corridor which no amount of cleaning will rid of the smell of urine and souring food. Some children wear face masks, another attempt by their parents to protect them from sickness and harm, the motive which brought them to Bulgaria in the first place.

To some extent they have succeeded: in Bulgaria they are safe from snipers, bombs and tanks. But a pitiful existence in the European Union's poorest nation - which cannot provide clothes, food, medicine or even enough beds - is not why they risked their lives crossing mountains.

"They put us here and there is no money," says Bangeen, who worked as a driver in Syria before fleeing first to Turkey, then into Bulgaria with his wife and three young children. "All the kids are sick. There is a lot of dust. It is dirty, and there are 10 families in a room."

Bangeen and many other refugees in Bulgaria carry a message for Europe's leaders, who have put off discussing an overhaul of the bloc's asylum policy until next June and are quietly hoping that the two million Syrian refugees will stay in Turkey, Jordan and Lebanon.

But the evidence in Bulgaria suggests otherwise. As Syria's war shows no sign of ending, people want a more permanent home than a tent in the desert. Nearly 8,000 men, women and children have arrived in Bulgaria so far this year - up from 2,000 last year. And they are not planning on building their lives here.

"No way, no one will stay here," says 23-year-old English language student Mazen Mustafa, who is aiming for Germany or Austria. "You see the situation here. It is too bad. If we get our travel documents, we will leave this country."

Voenna Rampa School was not meant to house the 800 people living here today. It was a communist-era woodwork academy and was closed decades ago. But Bulgaria has the facilities to house only 5,000 asylumseekers nationwide, so when Sofia's Migrant Reception Centre and other official sites filled up, they looked elsewhere.

There was hardly any time to repair the derelict building before the Syrians moved in. For the first few weeks, there was no hot water. That has been fixed, but no one has yet cleared the shattered glass from the yard where children play, or repaired the broken windows. There are only a few toilets for the hundreds of residents, and stomach bugs spread quickly.

Under EU law, member states must guarantee "a dignified standard of living" to people seeking refuge. It does not specify what constitutes such a life, but sleeping in rows of camp beds in a room with up to 50 other people does not appear to offer much dignity. Women from conservative Muslim families share a room with men they are not related to; some people sleep on blankets on the hard corridor floor.

"It is not meant to be a camp. This is not a hotel - it is a school," says camp commander Pepy Dzurenov. He lists overcrowding, unreliable food supplies and rudimentary health care as the main problems. But help is hard to come by. "Everything here is about the money." Bulgaria simply does not have the capacity to look after its new guests. It cannot even feed them. All food and clothing are provided by the Red Cross and other charities, which are relying on donations from ordinary Bulgarians, philanthropic business people and the local Muslim community.

Lack of medicine and doctors is a big problem. Many of the refugees are arriving with long--term illness, or injuries sustained in the war.

Ahmad Maruan Sahed, 23, was shot by a sniper near his home in a Palestinian refugee camp in Syria. The bullet shattered his hip, and his mother sent him to Europe with medical records and a doctor's recommendations that he undergo surgery to correct his heavy limp. There is no one to look at those papers at the Sofia Reception Centre, where he sleeps on a folding camp bed in a room with eight other men. He borrowed money to buy the medication he needs for the pain and his high blood pressure, but that will run out soon. Bulgaria cannot help him, so he appeals to the EU. "Take me to another country to get medical attention," he said. "Have some humanity."

Calls for more humanity from EU governments reached a peak last month, when 330 Somalis and Eritreans drowned off the coast of Italy while trying to reach Europe. A week later, dozens of Syrians died in a similar shipwreck between Malta and Italy. Human rights groups want the EU to provide more legitimate ways for asylum--seekers to reach safe havens without risking their lives. But with anti--immigrant parties expected to do well in European Parliament elections in May, there is little appetite for such a debate. Governments are instead reinforcing their borders. One reason Syrians are flooding into Bulgaria at a rate of up to 100 a day is because Greece last year completed a fence along much of its border with Turkey. Bulgaria is doing the same soon. This means Syrians fleeing war will have to find another route into Europe, most likely on the dangerous sea passage. Bulgaria has now joined Malta and Italy in asking for more EU money for the refugees, whose numbers are expected to swell to at least 11,000 by the end of the year. An EU official said emergency funds and logistical support would be made available, but added: "It is for them to fulfil their international and EU obligations on asylum."

Iliana Savova, a director at the Bulgaria Helsinki Committee human rights group, says the Bulgarian government should have foreseen the influx and been better prepared. She cautions the rest of Europe against making the same mistake.

"The neighbouring countries are hosting such a big population of Syrian refugees in such big camps," she says. "You can't live a normal life in a camp, [so] it's no wonder that even if 10 per cent of this population starts to move towards Europe, you have very big numbers."

Once the men and women get their refugee status, some will try to forge a life in Bulgaria. But with youth unemployment at nearly 30 per cent, the chance of a bright future is slim. "If this country is not providing the conditions, do expect them to come to your places," Ms Savova says. "I'm sorry, but that's the reality."

Charlotte McDonald-Gibson

11 November 2013

HUGE ARMIES OF HOMELESS AND BROKEN PEOPLE

The Syrian tragedy grows more ferocious by the week. I was shocked to learn this weekend that at least 2,000 Afghans, the poorest of the poor from the harshest country on earth - who fled the Soviet invasion of their land and then the post-Russian civil war and then the post-civil war Taliban and then the post-9/11 Taliban - are trapped in basements in Damascus, unable to flee Syria or return to their forlorn land. Theirs must be the most hideous nightmare, for most of them are Shia Muslims, despised by the Taliban and now by the Sunni rebels trying to overthrow Bashar al-Assad's government.

Since Assad is an Alawite, which is a form of Shiism, these Afghans are regarded as pro-regime by the Syrian opposition and accused of siding with the government. At least 10, I'm told, have been killed by car bombs and bullets. Most live around one building and the United Nations High Commissioner for Refugees knows of them - but when 10 families volunteered to leave two weeks ago and return to Afghanistan, the UN told them it could not assist their passage or guarantee their safety. Now this miserable community is appealing to the generosity of Canada to help them.

"We are with neither side of the hostile parties in Syria," one of them has written from Damascus. "We came here to solely survive the war which was going on in our native country." Perhaps Canada can save them. Certainly the rebels will not. Nor can I see the regime, fighting its way across the ruins of Syria, caring for their lives now. The Lebanese have now taken so many hundreds of thousands of Syrian refugees, they are unlikely to open their borders to Afghans. Do we care about them? Will Canada? I cannot help but be astonished at the vast population movements across the Middle East. In the 1970s and 1980s the Afghans were pouring in their millions across the Pakistani and Iranian borders. Tens of thousands of Lebanese regularly fled their civil war into Syria. Then in 1990, tens of thousands of Kuwaitis fled across their border from Saddam's invasion - followed by a Biblical exodus of Kurds towards Turkey. Then millions of Iraqis fled their homes after America's 2003 invasion and poured into Syria and Iran. And now the Syrians are living in their hundreds of thousands in

Lebanon: a quarter of Lebanon's population. In some mountain villages above Beirut, local authorities have even declared a curfew on the streets for Syrians.

They now beg on almost every street in the centre of the capital. Aggressive shoeshine boys haunt the Corniche outside my home. "From Syria," one said to me at the weekend, pointing to his filthy clothes and demanding money and pursuing me down the street, grabbing at my shirt. Of course, I gave him money. Syrian women sit now at the street corners, filthy children beside them, pleading for even a few Lebanese coins. The Lebanese economy groans under the weight of the huge camps opened along the border for the refugees. They are crossing now in vast numbers into northern Iraq and a giant city-camp exists for them in Jordan.

And I find myself wondering what catastrophic effect these mass migrations are having on the Middle East, destroying whole societies, ripping up tribal and family identities, turning the peoples of the Muslim (and Christian) world into huge armies of homeless and broken people. What effect does this have on religion, on their faith? Almost without recognizing it, we are faced with what must be the largest migration of souls across frontiers since the refugee treks which followed the end of the Second World War.

That conflict, too, was followed by misery and hunger and disease. Unsurprisingly, polio has broken out in Syria and 20 million children are to be vaccinated across the entire Middle East, from Turkey down to Gaza and Egypt. But now Egypt is giving Syrian refugees a rough time. Favoured by Mohamed Morsi - before the army chucked him out - Syrian refugees could access Egyptian healthcare and education. Morsi, of course, supported the rebels in Syria and broke off relations with Assad - one reason, perhaps, why the US smiled upon him - although the Americans may not have noticed his relationship with the Syrian Muslim Brotherhood.

But within days of the military coup in Cairo the so-called "interim" government now in place brought immigration restrictions back, and the Egyptian press, as lickspittle now as it was during Mubarak's heyday, began a campaign against both Palestinians and Syrian refugees, claiming that the Syrians had supported Morsi. One media presenter, as Cairo researcher Jasmin Fritzsche has pointed out, has even demanded that Egyptians destroy the homes and shops of Syrians if they did not withdraw their support from Morsi.

What is this vast brutalisation, the streams of refugees over the past decades - and here we must remember the 750,000 Palestinians whose lands were taken by the new Israel more than 60 years ago and whose descendants live in the filth of camps to this day - going to do to the region? They wash up in the seas off Australia or die in the Mediterranean, or struggle across Turkey in the hope of reaching Europe. They are people-smuggled, reduced to starvation, raped. What new harshness of spirit will spring from all this torment? Sweden perhaps understands this with its generosity towards the Syrians. Maybe Canada will help the Afghans of Damascus. But I fear the world, scarcely blameless amid all this sorrow, will close its borders tighter and blame the victims for their own desperation and throw at them some cash - as I did last week scarcely a hundred metres from my Beirut home - in the hope they will go away.

Robert Fisk

2014

MOUNTING HUMAN TOLL

Dunkirk refugee camp Grande-Synthe, France, 23 January 2016

18 January 2014

ALL I CAN THINK OF IS MY FAMILY I LEFT BEHIND

Today the former university student lives in Manchester, having made his way to Britain after escaping from Syria last summer. His family are still living in his battered hometown of Aleppo in north Syria - at least he can only assume this is the case, as hasn't been able to contact them in more than a year.

The Government says Britain has already granted asylum to 1,500 Syrian refugees. Many of these will either have already been in the UK as students or, like Syamend, have faced a dangerous journey across Europe in the hands of people smugglers. It is out of desire to prevent similar treacherous experiences, and to relieve the pressure on the refugee camps, that aid agencies are calling on Britain to join other nations in offering a systematic rehousing scheme for a number of refugees.

Speaking through an interpreter, he told The Independent he was "in danger" after he saw "bodies of people who had been killed by knife in front of me on the streets of Damascus".

He said: "There is no one who lives in Syria who hasn't seen dead bodies in the streets. Wherever people gather or demonstrate they are being targeted"

After a spate of bombings near his university, Syamend overcame his fear and convinced himself he had to leave and head for Turkey. He ended up living in cramped conditions with "hundreds of families, no job and little food" at a Turkish camp. Sick of the "terrible conditions" and harsh treatment, he managed to bribe a people smuggler to get him to Greece. The sea crossing was made in a tiny inflatable boat which capsized in sight of the shore, throwing Syamend and 20 others, some as young as five, into the water only 500 metres from the safety of the Europe Union.

They were rescued by Greek coastguards before being finger-printed and photographed. They were also threatened, he claims, with being returned to Turkey. He said: "No one died in my dinghy but I know other families who undertook the journey and didn't make it."

After contacting a "distant cousin" who had also fled Syria he was able to secure "false papers" and "a little money", letting him make his way to France before catching the ferry to Dover in August 2013.

Now settled, to some degree, in Manchester, he visits the office of the charity Refugee Action every week for support and advice. He still doesn't know the fate of his parents, three brothers and five sisters in war-torn Aleppo, and can only hope the messages he has sent friends in the region have made it to them.

Syamend, who was granted leave to remain in September, said: "There is nothing worse than being uprooted; nothing could hurt more than being separated from your family, knowing they're at risk. It feels as if my heart is being ripped from my chest."

He is convinced he can never return to Syria. "For now, I can't think of the future - of Syria's future. All I can think of is my family."

Jamie Merrill

6 February 2014

VICTIM OF THE DUBLIN REGULATION

When Muhammed Hatif fled Syria he never thought he would end up in a British detention centre. Today, however, the 25-year-old refugee is among a group of his compatriots facing deportation from Britain to eastern Europe. Their numbers may be small, but they are vulnerable, and frightened.

Formerly a reluctant soldier for the Assad regime, Muhammed left his native Aleppo for Turkey in September 2012 with the aim of reaching "safety" in Britain, where he says he has cousins.

He paid people smugglers to get him to Hungary - where he says was beaten and kept in solitary confinement - before continuing on his journey through Austria, Italy and France, arriving in Dover on the back of a lorry in July 2013 and quickly being detained.

Like other Syrians in British custody he is facing a return to eastern Europe under the EU's controversial Dublin regulation - which allows member states to return asylum seekers to the first European country they entered - despite the Government moving to accept 500 Syrian refugees after a campaign by aid agencies and The Independent.

Refugee charities and human rights bodies, including Amnesty International UK, Human Rights Watch, Refugee Action and the Refugee Council, have condemned the British Government practice of detaining and returning some Syrian refugees. Muhammed said he is "terrified" of being returned to "squalid conditions" and "poor treatment" in Hungary, where he will likely have to be returned. Speaking through an interpreter, he described how he was detained in Hungary on his arrival last year and was kept in solitary confinement, "punched like a boxer's bag" by police, "stripped naked" and only fed once a day until he agreed to provide his fingerprints to asylum authorities. The Independent was unable to verify all of Muhammed's claims, but charities suggest his tale is not unusual.

Jerome Phelps, director of Detention Action, said that "traumatised people are facing removal to third countries where conditions are very poor" and that they are "being detained in a prison-like environment in the UK beforehand".

Muhammed said he was disappointed with Britain and had not expect to be "treated like a criminal".

Human Rights Watch and Amnesty International UK have condemned the failure to sufficiently reform the controversial Dublin regulation and raised concerns over conditions for refugees returned to countries on the border of the EU, including Bulgaria, Italy, Greece and Hungary.

A recent Amnesty International report also highlighted UNHCR's concerns over Hungary's treatment of asylum seekers. The country accepted 18,000 Syrian refugees last year but there have been reports of poor conditions in reception centres and reports that conditions in detention fall short of international and EU standards.

The Home Office says individuals are only detained if there is a realistic prospect of their removal, but has refused to rule out the return of Syrians under the Dublin Regulation. A spokesperson added: "The UK has a proud history of granting asylum to those who need it. All asylum cases are considered on their individual merits and in line with immigration rules."

Jamie Merrill

16 May 2014

EUROPE'S REFUGEE DEATH SENTENCE

Last October, EU leaders, united in their shock after at least 350 migrants drowned off the Italian coast, promised action. Yet seven months on, there are fears that the waters of the Mediterranean could again turn into a graveyard this summer, with the EU home affairs chief warning that governments must start finding legal ways to get desperate people to Europe - or risk more tragedy.

"Pathetically few" nations in Europe have stepped forward to offer a safe haven to desperate Syrian refugees, Cecilia Malmstrom, the European Commissioner for Home Affairs, has told The Independent, raising the risk that many more could die at sea as they instead embark on perilous journeys to seek sanctuary.

Her warning came as the EU's border agency, Frontex, reported a leap in the number of people detected entering Europe illegally this year, with Syrians making up the largest proportion. Up to half a million people are also believed to be massing in Libya and preparing to cross the Mediterranean, a route which claimed more than 700 lives last year.

Despite signs that the situation could worsen, agencies trying to save lives are having to contend with shrinking budgets, a political vacuum in Libya and xenophobic rhetoric from far-right parties which has seeped into government refugee policy.

Ms Malmstrom said she hopes there will be more boats patrolling the Mediterranean this summer, and praised the efforts of the Italian coastguard, which earlier this week came ashore with 200 survivors and 17 bodies from the latest wreck.

But she said the tragedies will not stop until people are given the chance to get to Europe safely and legally. "Why do people embark on those boats? Because there are no legal ways to get to Europe. The immediate way to help people, especially people from Syria, would be to engage in resettlement," she said. "Pathetically few countries take resettled refugees."

Ms Malmstrom said 14 European countries have so far refused to resettle any Syrians refugees, giving excuses ranging from financial hardship to pressure from far-right parties, whose support has surged in reaction to unemployment, austerity and the euro crisis. "I would have hoped for stronger political leadership in all countries to stand up against those forces," said Ms Malmstrom, adding that the European Commission had no power over governments' migration policy and could not force nations to house the refugees.

"I can only appeal to the humanitarian side of people. These are people who really need support, and if you can take some of the most vulnerable children in a safe way to your country, they don't have to embark on these rickety vessels and maybe drown."

She praised the British Government's decision to take in 500 of the most vulnerable Syrians, which followed a campaign by The Independent. Other nations offering sanctuary include Sweden, Norway, Germany and France. But a list complied by the EU's Eurostat agency showed no pledges from Poland, Croatia, Estonia and Slovakia. While rehousing a few hundred refugees barely makes a dent when 2.7 million have fled the civil war, Ms Malmstrom said it is "better than zero".

The indications are that many more will be trying to reach Europe this summer. Frontex, which monitors and helps to patrol the EU land and sea borders, reported a 48 per cent jump in migrant arrivals between 2012 and 2013. The largest numbers came from Syria and Eritrea, both countries blighted by conflict and human rights abuses. So far this year, 42,000 people have been recorded entering the EU illegally - most of them in Italy. That is up from 12,400 in the same period last year.

Most crossings are attempted in the summer months when the water is calmer and reports in the Italian press suggest that at least half a million people could be poised to attempt the journey soon. This has prompted the Libyan government to demand more money from the EU, with one politician threatening that they could "facilitate" the migrants' journeys. Ms Malmstrom called such statements "disgraceful", but conceded that the lack of any stable government to work with in Libya was a huge problem.

Nations including Bulgaria, Italy and Malta have also pleaded for more EU funding to deal with increasing numbers of refugees, but governments are stretched. Gil Arias-Fernandez, deputy executive director of Frontex, said its budget for 2014 was slightly lower than in 2013. Another problem plaguing Europe's borders are accusations that security forces are expelling people before processing their asylum claims. These "pushbacks" are illegal under international law but human rights groups have accused Greece and Bulgaria of the practice.

"I am convinced that it is happening," Ms Malmstrom said. But without any powers to go and investigate the claims, she said there was little the EU could do short of asking the member states for an explanation and threatening to cut funding.

This is a recurring problem for the European Commission. Because border control and migration are such toxic domestic issues, the EU has been granted few competencies in the area. Many of the people risking their lives are trying to get to Europe to work and Ms Malmstrom is convinced that opening up more legal routes to apply for jobs in the EU would stem the deaths at sea and be an economic benefit for member states. She will be pushing this policy at a meeting of EU leaders in June but she is not optimistic.

In the short term, Ms Malmstrom is hoping that a new EU-wide informationsharing system known as Eurosur should help. In theory, governments and naval forces share intelligence and real-time satellite images to detect boats of migrants that might be at risk of sinking. But Mr Fernandez said that the system relies on member states uploading information quickly and so far, "this does not fulfil this service".

Judith Sunderland, a researcher with Human Rights Watch, said it was essential that the EU get this fully operational immediately. "Without that commitment the coming months could be the drowning season," she said.

Charlotte McDonald-Gibson

17 June 2014

'FLOTSAM OF A WRECKED WORLD'

How do you like your broccoli? In an interview ahead of a 2012 BBC series on poverty, the director Nick Fraser said that trying to get people to watch documentaries that deal with human suffering was not too different from trying to feed them the notorious vegetable. Its health benefits are well-known. But the world is full of the televised equivalent of crème caramel and - when you've got your own problems to digest - it can be daunting to sit down to a plate stacked tall with the green stuff, or in Mr Fraser's case, a series of films that explore the structural nature of poverty.

Two details plucked from the tide of news surrounding Europe's migration crisis have served me a portion over the past month or so. They take place against a backdrop of stomach-evacuating misery.

More than half-a-million people wait on the shores of North Africa for a smuggler's boat to take them into Europe. Many of them are fleeing Syria's civil war. Already, Italy has picked up 50,000 seaborne migrants this year - more than the entire total in 2013. On Friday the UN High Commissioner for Refugees pleaded with northern EU states to take in more of the migrants who arrive in Italy and Greece. Currently southern nations are left to bear the cost of what The Economist referred to as "the flotsam of a wrecked world".

This is patently unjust. That faraway Britain has admitted just 24 Syrian refugees through its resettlement programme, launched in January, is a stain on this nation's tradition of offering safe haven to those fleeing war (last week Germany committed to take in a further 10,000). All of this, however, simply points to the scale of the crisis. It induces anger in numerical terms. Unless you holiday in Lampedusa, those numbers are unlikely to resolve into individual human beings.

So the details matter. My first is this. On the weekend a Calais security guard used an air rifle with a telescopic sight to shoot two immigrants apparently en route to Britain. They were hit in the back and the arm. The shooting captures a hostility bordering on rage in elements of native European populations - and the cruelty of many attempts to shore up national borders.

Second was the poem shared around the Eritrean online diaspora following the death of more than 300 migrants off the coast of Lampedusa last October. A woman and her new-born child were among the dead. Where an image would have scalded the mind, the elegy comes at a cooler, though no less devastating, temperature: "His mother feebly fighting to stay afloat / A baby boy was born / No one saw his eyes / Open briefly / Then shut".

The EU is considering setting up offices in Africa to process the claims of asylum-seekers before they risk their lives at sea. That is sensible. Fortress Europe cannot keep ignoring the corpses at its door.

Memphis Barker

5 September 2014

CALAIS MIGRANTS

Sibatu says he is 18 years old. He looks 20 years older. After travelling "with many problems" 3,000 miles from Eritrea, he has spent the past six months in the rain of the Channel coast a few miles from his destination.

On Wednesday evening he was among 200 would-be asylum-seekers - mostly young East African men - who tried to storm a cross-Channel ferry in the port of Calais.

"The others told me this is the only way," he told The Independent yesterday. "Maybe, a few of us could get on a boat. Maybe none. We didn't win this time. We will try again."

After 20 years of deadlock, the never-ending saga of the Calais migrants is threatening to explode into outright crisis. The Mayor of Calais, Natacha Bouchart, spoke this week of shutting the port unless the British Government does more to help. She says her town has been "taken hostage" by the 1,300 migrants sleeping rough in the day and trying to board lorries - and now ships - by night. Relations between the two main categories of migrants - refugees from Africa and the Middle East - are increasingly tense. A far right march is planned on Sunday to demand that all the migrants should be systematically arrested and kicked out of France. Wednesday's mass trespass through the main gates of the Calais ferry port is described by French police as a "worrying change in tactics".

Until now, the migrants have mostly haunted approach roads and attempted to stow away in British-bound lorries or climb on to their back axles. Catherine Konforti, president of a charitable group which feeds the Calais migrants, said: "It was just desperation. After months of failing to get on lorries, they were desperate to try something new." This week the French government bowed to pressure from the United Nations and announced plans to open a day centre - strictly non-residential - where the migrants can eat, shower and receive medical help. This is a significant change of policy after 12 years of harassment and the bulldozing of squatter camps.

The new centre will be the first official refuge since British pressure forced the closure of the Red Cross residential camp at Sangatte, just south of Calais, in 2002. It will inevitably be branded a "new Sangatte" by the right-wing press and politicians in Britain.

The French government and Ms Bouchart say the problem is partly of Britain's making. She and the Interior Minister Bernard Cazeneuve want the Government to pay towards policing the port (which costs France €10m a year). They also want Britain to persuade refugees that the UK is not the El Dorado painted by people-smugglers.

For almost 20 years, Calais has attracted an ever-changing cast of the stricken or the enterprising from Europe, Asia, the Middle East and now Africa. The problem began in 1994-5 with Bosnian refugees. The 1,300 migrants in Calais represent a mini-United Nations of conflict and oppression. About one in five are from countries such as Syria, Afghanistan and Pakistan. The great majority - and this is a relatively new development - are from Eritrea, Somalia, Darfur and the rest of Sudan.

There was a street-battle last month between the Africans and Middle Eastern group over the right to exploit the most prized sections of the slip-roads approaching the ferry port. In an attempt to deflate tensions, welfare groups have organised an Africa vs. The Rest migrants' football match this Sunday.

Why do they not apply for asylum in France or simply vanish into the French black economy? This is a complex issue and one frequently misrepresented in Britain.

Sibatu said: "I go to England because in Eritrea there is only violence. In England, I have Eritrean friends who will get me a job, a new
life."

Why not apply for political asylum in France? "I no speak French.
I have no friends in France." Another Eitrean, Jemal, 21, said he had
tried the official asylum route in France and got nowhere. "So now I'll
try and go to England because the people there are friendly. I can get
a job there."

Tens of thousands of illegal migrants enter France every year.
The majority want to stay in France. Some, especially the Afghans, Syrians and Pakistanis, come to France only to reach Britain. An
increasing number, especially the Eritreans, emigrate to Europe without any country in mind. They are poorly treated in Italy and France
and head for the Channel coast.

The Calais problem is acute, and visible, because Britain is an island and does not belong to the EU open-borders Schengen
Agreement.

Ms Bouchart and Mr Cazeneuve say Britain can no longer pretend
this is just a "French problem". Under agreements reached in 2009
and 2010, Britain pays for body-heatdetecting equipment and other
control measures.

In a meeting last week with the Home Secretary, Theresa May, Mr
Cazeneuve asked Britain to cover more of the cost of security and welfare. He asked her to send officials to tell the migrants Britain was a
cold, wet island where illegal jobs are hard to come by.

In return, the French minister promised to prosecute migrants
caught stowing away and to send them home. In practise, the systematic expulsion of migrants to war zones is opposed by French courts
on human rights grounds.

The mayor's threat to close the ferry port should probably not be
taken seriously either. The town's economy depends on British visitors.

With a British election approaching, it is equally unlikely that Ms
May will give ground (or money). Crisis or no crisis, the 20-year deadlock continues.

John Lichfield

21 November 2014

TIGHTER SECURITY WON'T SOLVE CALAIS PROBLEM

One is France's fourthbusiest port and the other is the capital of a small African nation scarred by poverty and repression.

Yet it is impossible to separate the fates of Calais and Asmara, cities divided by more than 3,200 miles, as the misery of everyday life in Eritrea is in stark evidence across the English Channel.

Eritreans - so desperate to reach Britain that they have journeyed across the Sahara, the Mediterranean and Europe - make up about half of the migrants leaving in squalor in Calais. They are joined by other Africans as well as Syrians and Afghans fleeing from the violence in their homelands.

Hundreds of migrants linger every day near the freight terminal in the hope that they can smuggle themselves on to a lorry bound for the UK, with their frustrations occasionally boiling over into clashes with police.

Some find themselves in the grip of Albanian gangs which run lucrative peoplesmuggling operations across Europe with many migrants seduced by illusory promises of riches awaiting them in Britain. Dealing with the crisis at Calais has become one of the biggest problems confronting the Home Secretary, Theresa May, and James Brokenshire, her immigration minister. Labour points to the chaos as evidence of the Coalition's failure to police Britain's frontiers and promises to recruit more border staff.

The migrants' living conditions, which have been compared with the world's most wretched refugee camps, have also developed into a headache for the French government, which is under fire domestically for allowing a humanitarian catastrophe to develop.

Britain's response has been to pledge £12m over three years to tighten security at the freight terminal. Much of the money is being spent on moving the 9ft-high fences which guarded the world's leaders at the recent NATO summit in Newport to Calais.

The port will also be reconfigured to improve the flow of traffic and reduce the number of stationary vehicles targeted by migrants. However, if the measures work and the terminal is turned into a fortress which repels all migrants, the problem would be displaced rather than solved.

Migrants head for Calais because of the frequency of ferry sailings, but they could easily gather in other French or Belgian ports perceived as a softer touch.

There have been warnings they could try to jump into the cars of tourists returning to Dover and even run into the Channel tunnel.

They could resort to other, and potentially riskier, ways of getting to Britain: in August a man died when he was among 35 Afghans crammed into a sealed container shipped from Zeebrugge to Tilbury.

The real solution, politicians and transport chiefs alike agree, is to tackle the problem at source, a far more daunting challenge than erecting security fences or hiring extra border officers.

Mr Brokenshire travels to Rome next week to help launch a fresh EU attempt to find ways of easing the migratory pressures from Eritrea and neighbouring Somalia and Ethiopia as well as tackling the trafficking gangs in Libya and Egypt.

He says: "Calais is just one very visible sign of a much wider problem. It often has its roots in the Horn of Africa, where people first make the decision to risk their lives on the perilous journey to Europe."

It will be a painfully difficult and slow process, though, to identify methods to bring stability to a region which has been in turmoil for decades - and thus reduce ambitious young citizens' desire to leave.

More than ever we live in an inter-connected, shrinking world and no amounts of fearsome barriers at Calais will alter that.

The real solution is to tackle the problem at source, a far more daunting challenge.

Nigel Morris

January 2015

RAPACIOUS TRAFFICKERS

Italian Coast Guard, Palermo, Italy, 22 October 2014

3 January 2015

GHOST SHIP WITH A HUMAN CARGO

The Italian Coast Guard was last night towing the second un-manned ship containing hundreds of migrants to appear off its coast this week into port. The so-called "ghost ships" are a worrying new trend as human traffickers exploit desperate refugees bidding for a new life in Europe.

The Lebanese vessel Ezadeen, which was discovered with about 450 passengers on board, is registered as a livestock vessel. But even cattle are not left to cross dangerous high seas in mid-winter with no crew and the vessel on autopilot.

Coast Guard officers boarded the Ezadeen from a helicopter yesterday morning and navigated it towards Corigliano Calabro where it was due to arrive late last night.

The practice of using "ghost ships" - filling rust buckets with refugees, pointing the vessel towards Italy and then fleeing with the passengers' life-savings - appears to be a worrying new development in human trafficking, the UN's refugee agency, the UNHCR, warned yesterday.

The rescue of the Ezadeen follows a similar operation to save hundreds of migrants aboard another abandoned ship, the Blue Sky M, on Wednesday.

"We are seeing this new trend. It's apparent there have been other such incidents - maybe four or five in the past two months," said UNHCR spokesman William Spindler.

"But only when the Blue SkyM incident occurred this week, which involved nearly 1,000 people, did it capture everyone's attention."

Mr Spindler said it showed that human traffickers were changing tactics. "They're using bigger boats and different routes to smuggle people. "In the past they have come from Libya in dinghies and boats, but that route seems to have been closed by Frontex [the EU's border agency]."

Admiral Giovanni Pettorino of the Italian Coast Guard said that by charging hundreds of desperate refugees thousands of dollars at a time, gangs in North Africa and the Middle East were still able to make big profits by writing off ageing ships in the process of smuggling human beings.

"They purchase unseaworthy vessels for $100,000 to $150,000 (£65,000 to £97,000) and then fill them with hundreds of migrants, mainly Syrian nationals, who pay $6,000 each for the crossing from the Turkish coast to Europe," said Admiral Pettorino.

He told the Adnkronos news agency that the criminals were netting up to $5m per trip and therefore "had no hesitation about jumping ship, given the profit margins".

Last month the UNHCR described the Mediterranean crossing from the Middle East and Africa to Europe as "the most lethal route in the world" after a record 3,419 migrants lost their lives in 2014 crossing the sea.

Although it has not been confirmed where the migrants aboard the Ezadeen come from, the UNHCR told The Independent it believed the number of refugees from Syria was rising sharply.

In 2014 for the first time, people from refugee-producing countries - mainly Syria and Eritrea (as opposed to countries producing high numbers of economic migrants) - "have become a major component in this tragic flow, accounting for almost 50 per cent of the total", said the UN body. On Wednesday about 900, mostly Syrian, refugees arrived in Italy after they were abandoned by the crew of the Moldovan-registered Blue Sky M cargo ship, who had fled leaving the vessel on a crash course for the Italian coast. The Coast Guard also boarded that vessel and navigated it to port.

The Blue Sky M drifted within five miles of the shore before six navy officers were lowered on to the ship by helicopter and succeeded in bringing it under control.

One migrant aboard the 48-year-old Ezadeen, which is registered in Sierra Leone but has Lebanese owners, managed to operate the vessel's radio and contact the Italian Coast Guard on Thursday night.

By this point the ship's crew had fled, leaving it to plough a course. The Coast Guard notified the nearby Icelandic patrol boat Tyr, which was in the area on a mission with Frontex. The Tyr drew alongside the runaway ship, but huge waves made boarding impossible.

A Frontex spokesman said: "It was not until some hours later, when the vessel carrying the migrants ran out of fuel, that five Icelandic officers were able to get on board, attach a tow rope and bring the ship under control."

Yesterday, six Italian Coast Guard officers were lowered from a helicopter on to the deck of the 73m-long Ezadeen to take control and navigate the vessel to the Italian mainland.

Frontex said the migrants aboard were "visibly distressed but overall in good medical condition". They have been given food, water and basic medical assistance.

Coast Guard spokesman Filippo Marini said the nationality or nationalities of the migrants was not yet clear.

He added: "What is clear is that among them there were lots of children and women, including some pregnant women. What we know for now is that the ship left from a Turkish port and that the crew fled."

Michael Day

February 2015

'MOST PRESSING HUMAN DISASTER OF OUR TIME'

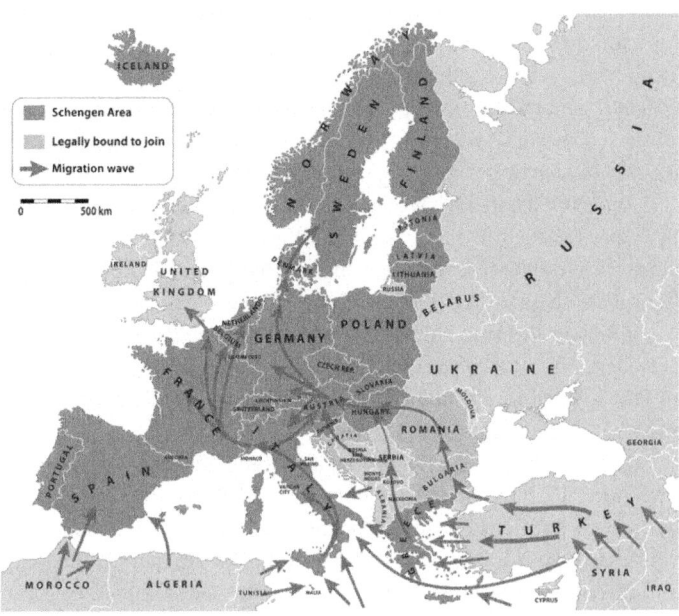

Migration waves through the Schengen Area, 2016

8 February 2015

FOUR MILLION REFUGEES ABANDONED

For a certain generation, images of desperate Syrian refugees crammed into overcrowded boats carrying their children in their arms may seem familiar. In the late 1970s, after the fall of Saigon (now Ho Chi Minh City), a similar exodus of Vietnamese fleeing the new

Communist regime created the first wave of people who were willing to risk death at sea to find safety and sanctuary for their families.

Many succumbed to piracy, drowning or dehydration, but those who made it alive filled refugee camps in Thailand, Malaysia, Indonesia and Hong Kong. Like the ripple effect from the Syrian refugee crisis today, neighbouring countries were overwhelmed and appealed for help.

Back then, the world responded: between 1975 and 1995 around 1.3 million refugees were resettled across the West. Today, the world faces its biggest refugee crisis since the Second World War and nearly four million Syrians languish in camps in Turkey, Lebanon and Jordan. They have fled a conflict that has claimed the lives of more than 210,000 people, half of them civilians, according to figures from the UK-based Syrian Observatory for Human Rights. The group, which has a network of activists across Syria, says the figure could be far higher.

Developed nations have so far pledged sanctuary to just 104,000 Syrian refugees. Now there are calls for a similar scheme to the Indochina resettlement programme to stop Syrians and others risking their lives on boats in the Mediterranean.

François Crépeau, the United Nations Special Rapporteur for migrants' rights, is calling on countries in Europe, and other rich nations, to find homes for one million refugees over five years through an organised and fair quota system.

"We can do it - we did it for the Indochinese 30 years ago, we can do it now," he told The Independent on Sunday. "There is not this eagerness to do the right thing that there was at that time, but states could say that it is our responsibility and have the moral leadership and the political courage They can make the case, taking the risk of losing [votes], but taking a stand and telling the population, 'It's not necessarily easy, it's not necessarily what you want, but it's what you have to do.'" So far, only Germany and Sweden have stood up to rising antiimmigrant forces within their countries and launched significant resettlement programmes for Syrians. The response of the rest of Europe has been derided by human rights experts, with Britain being singled out for its reaction. Despite a pledge from David Cameron one year ago that the Government would respond with "urgency", only 90 Syrian refugees have been offered sanctuary.

Jan Shaw, Amnesty International UK's refugee expert, said: "The Syrian refugee crisis has been called the most pressing humanitarian disaster of our time, yet the response by the international community has, with very few exceptions, been pitiful. You only need to look to the history books to see how nations working together can be effective in alleviating these crises. How many more Vietnamese or Kosovars would have been killed, tortured or raped if the international community hadn't come together to offer them safety?" The Indochina crisis began after the fall of Saigon in 1975, when a steady stream of Vietnamese fled persecution from the new Communist regime. The numbers increased as repressive governments took hold in Laos and Cambodia, with three million people fleeing, many by boat, over two decades.

Under a new framework for Syrian and Eritrean refugees envisaged by Mr Crépeau, people could apply for resettlement from the camps in neighbouring countries. They would be allocated to host nations under a quota system which would take into account population, GDP, available land, and population density. Mr Crépeau estimates that would mean a nation like Canada would take 9,000 Syrians a year, while Germany would re-house 20,000 per year. "These are not huge numbers once you distribute them by year and by country according to a distribution key," he said.

The impact for those fleeing war, however, would be huge, with people no longer compelled to take to the Mediterranean on a migration route on which least 3,000 people were killed last year.

Mr Crépeau acknowledges a different climate today compared with the Indochina refugee crisis. Politicians are battling a rise in support for anti-immigration, nationalist and far-right parties, and any policies bringing more people into European countries are considered toxic.

The Indochina refugee crisis was also drawn out over decades, and came at a time when images of desperate people crammed on to boats still had the power to shock. "That was horrifying, because that was on TV in colour, and it created a huge emotional appeal which we don't have for the Syrians," Mr Crépeau said. He also concedes that the European Union is constantly beset by bickering, so reaching agreement on any quota system "is going to be hell".

Which is perhaps why many organisations are looking at less ambitious targets. Amnesty has called on rich and developed countries to resettle 5 per cent of the Syrian refugees by the end of the year.

UNHCR wants to re-house the most vulnerable refugees, and has a target of 130,000 resettlement places.

But they agree more needs to be done to show solidarity with nations shouldering the burden of the refugees. "The Syrian war is the most dramatic humanitarian crisis of our time," said Ariane Rummery, a spokesperson for the UN refugee agency. "It calls for unprecedented measures."

Charlotte McDonald-Gibson

23 February 2015

MIGRANT DEATHS SHAME A CONTINENT

The statistics and stories are so extreme they barely register any more. In just five days, 4,200 migrants were plucked from nightmarishly full, rickety boats as they made the perilous trip across the Mediterranean - the equivalent of one person every two minutes.

Many had spent dangerous months crossing deserts, dodging lethal militias and then trusting lives to rapacious traffickers. But as they slept outside in soggy clothes on a mid-winter night having made the promised lands of Europe, they were the lucky ones.

For whatever their futures, at least they were alive. Dozens more drowned in those rough, icy waters, lonely deaths on the world's most lethal route for migrants. Their bodies lined an Italian harbour as hearses queued to take them to an old airport converted into a temporary morgue.

Another 29 people lost their lives after they had been rescued, dying of hypothermia on the decks of small coastguard vessels fighting valiantly to save them in extreme weather conditions.

But they are only Arabs and Africans, so their lives seem not to count for much in Europe. For that is the only conclusion that can be drawn from the cloud of silence over these ceaseless deaths as human beings risk everything in their search for the sort of stable lives taken for granted by people in Manchester, Milan or Munich.

Yet many of these unfortunates might still be alive today were it not for crass political expediency in a climate of fear over immigration.

Four months ago Foreign Office minister Baroness Anelay announced Britain would not support search and rescue missions to stop migrants drowning in the Mediterranean.

The justification was simple: such services only encourage desperate people to make the treacherous trip. "We believe that they create an unintended pull factor, encouraging more migrants to attempt the dangerous sea crossing and thereby leading to more tragic and unnecessary deaths," she told the House of Lords.

This sounded a spurious argument to cover a callous decision of astonishing inhumanity, rightly condemned by Labour leader Ed Miliband. And now we can see the stark evidence that proves this policy of supposed deterrence has failed since the end of Mare Nostrum, the Italian rescue operation that helped save an estimated 150,000 lives. It was replaced by Operation Triton, far more limited in scope with fewer and smaller boats patrolling only close to the shore, funded by just one-third of the budget. Just look at the disturbing data issued by the UN. In the first six weeks of this year the number of people known to have attempted the crossing more than doubled on the previous year, from 3,338 to more than 7,000.

This is bad enough. But far worse is the number of confirmed deaths, which soared from 12 over this same period last year to 373 this year - a rise of more than thirtyfold.

Among them were those 29 people who froze to their deaths as waves washed over them during an 18-hour rescue mission.

"If Mare Nostrum were still going, the migrants would have been given shelter inside a large ship within an hour," said Giusi Nicolini, mayor of Lampedusa, the Italian island on the front line of this crisis. But still the boats keep coming: from crammed plastic craft that should never attempt such a crossing to ghastly "ghost ships", those ancient rustbuckets abandoned by crews to leave their huddled human cargo helplessly drifting.

One UN source told me it was "nuts" to suggest there was a "pull factor", which is underlined by these depressing figures. We are, after all, living amid the greatest refugee crisis since the Second World War, with some 50 million people forced from their homes and worsening violence and repression sweeping across the Middle East and Sahel.

It stretches credibility to suggest that despairing people fleeing savage groups such as Isis and Boko Haram are pondering the standard of rescue services before paying small fortunes to smugglers to save their families and salvage wrecked lives.

Ask yourself what you might do, trapped in one of these horror stories, seeing security and prosperity just 70 miles away over the sea.

And as turmoil spreads in Libya, with the longest coastline of any southern Mediterranean country, this is a crisis that can only worsen.

Britain likes to pose as a force for decency in the world. But permitting hundreds of people to die is simply immoral, especially when driven by domestic politics and from a country that sent its forces into battle in two of the nations worst afflicted by bloodstained chaos.

Yes, the Government has given aid. But for all the fine talk, fewer than 100 of those fleeing the carnage have been permitted to come here under a scheme to protect Syrians most at risk. Germany, by contrast, agreed to take 30,000 - while some countries neighbouring Syria have seen populations swollen by almost a quarter.

The European Commission last week agreed extra funds to ensure Operation Triton keeps going until the end of the year. Sadly, it is still far too little and comes too late. These are, of course, immense challenges with no simple solutions. But this mammoth tide of human misery and desperation is not going to stop in the near future. So how will history judge this doomed attempt to pull up the drawbridge on Fortress Europe, regardless of all those corpses left floating in the sea like sordid human flotsam?

Ian Birrell

March 2015

UKHIP

Welcome to Calais roadsign

11 March 2015

'TURKEY'S MYSTERIOUS DISAPPEARING REFUGEES'

Turkey may be hosting far fewer than the 2.7 million Syrian refugees declared in official figures, according to a controversial new claim.

An article in an online magazine by an aid worker and a former aid worker argues that many of those registered as living in Turkey may already have left for Europe, while others may have been registered several times. The claim comes as European leaders prepare to thrash out the final details of a deal with Turkey designed to prevent a repeat of the influx of people who arrived in Europe last year.

Ankara drove a hard bargain at an emergency summit in Brussels this week. In return for agreeing to allow all refugees and migrants arriving in EU countries to be sent back to Turkey, the nation's Prime Minister, Ahmet Davutoglu, asked EU leaders to double a package of aid for Syrians in his country to €6bn (£4.7bn).

Questions about the actual numbers were raised in an article published on The Balkanist website under the headline "Turkey's mysterious disappearing refugees". Written by an aid official based in southern Turkey, who works for an unnamed organisation, and a former humanitarian worker, it cites figures showing that 880,000 people arrived in Greece last year after crossing by sea from Turkey. In the same period, the number of Syrian refugees reported as living in Turkey rose from 1.5 million to 2.5 million. The current total claimed by Ankara stands at 2.7 million.

For that increase to be accurate, the authors say, 80,000 refugees must have crossed into Turkey from Syria every month last year, excluding anyone who went straight to Europe. However, from about March last year it has become much harder for Syrians to cross into Turkey, as large sections of the border have been closed.

The article notes that the numbers of Syrians living in official government camps rose slightly in 2015 from 230,000 to 270,000.

The authors warn that the official Turkish figures are "being accepted uncritically by aid groups and government officials" when they should be treated with more caution - especiallywhen they form the basis of frantic EU negotiations.

A senior Turkish official did not deny that the figure for Syrians in Turkey could be too high, but said that it was "difficult to tell".

He told The Independent: "We don't know if 100 per cent of Syrians currently in Turkey are registered, even though the authorities have been trying very hard to register everyone. At the same time it is unclear how many people left - how many people drowned, or ended up in Europe." He suggested that the numbers in Europe could also be inaccurate because people who travelled to Germany or Sweden crossed many national borders and were reregistered and reported every time they did so.

All those arriving in Greece from Turkey are supposed to be registered, raising the prospect that they could, in theory, be crossed off against the list of names of refugees in Turkey.

Frontex, the EU border agency, has sent hundreds of officers, seconded from police forces across Europe, to help the Greek authorities record all new arrivals.

However, a spokesman for the agency said that information about individuals was passed only to the Greek authorities and could not be shared more widely because of data protection laws.

The numbers crossing the Aegean Sea have shown few signs of declining. More than 130,000 people have reached Europe from Turkey this year alone. Yesterday, two children and a six-month-old baby were among five Afghans who drowned trying to reach the Greek island of Lesbos.

Meanwhile, a group of 30 aid agencies has warned that the fifth year of the Syrian conflict was the worst so far, with civilians suffering from intensified violence, aid blockades and siege warfare. The charities, which include Oxfam, say that at least 50,000 people were killed over the past year.

They criticise Russia, the United States, France and Britain for undermining their own resolutions through "inadequate diplomatic pressure, political and military support to their allies or direct military action".

Laura Pitel

24 March 2015

'FLOTILLA OF SOLIDARITY'

When Beth Granville's grandmother, Liz, spotted a promotion in a newspaper in the new year, she cut it out. The "Sail to France from just £1!" offer included a day in Calais, and a free bottle of P&O wine. Liz knew that Beth and her friend, David Charles, had visited Calais before and thought they might enjoy another jaunt on the cheap.

She was right, but rather than stock up on duty-free booze, Charles and Granville used the Daily Mail's largesse to launch an unlikely humanitarian mission. Armed with blankets, food and goodwill, the writing partners headed to the camps and squats that have become a grim home to hundreds of refugees, many of whom have fled war only to be bombarded with prejudice and more poverty on the shores of northern France.

Charles then wrote a sarcastic letter on his blog, thanking the Mail for the opportunity to help migrants ("Your courageous human-itarian stance should be saluted..."). It went viral, inspiring like-minded sailors to make similar voyages, and this Saturday, the activ-ists are upping their game, with plans to lead an entire "flotilla of solidarity" to Calais.

"So far we know of at least 25 people who are coming, including half a cricket team," says Charles, 32. In a further attempt to bait those with less empathetic views of immigration, the writer is organising the operation under a new flag for a new party: The UK Humanitarian Intervention Party (Ukhip). Its purple and yellow logo might look fa-miliar, too. "Hopefully we're going to have a game with the Afghans," he adds. "They love cricket, and everyone wants to do something that isn't running away from the police or fascists." Humour is Ukhip's ve-hicle, but the party is driven by serious concern. Charles first crossed the Channel last summer after hearing about the work of Calais Mi-grant Solidarity. For five years the group has been a permanent presence in the port, supporting migrants, monitoring police activity and documenting deaths. In 2011, about 200 people were camped there, blocked from legal passage to Britain by immigration laws. By the end of last year, as war forced people to flee countries including Syria and Eritrea, that number has grown to more than 2,000. Last year, at least 15 people died in and around Calais, many while trying to board lorries in desperation. Meanwhile, UN observers have called conditions in the port "shameful".

Charles remembers meeting a man who had fled civil war in South Sudan, before surviving a terrorist carjacking en route to Libya and a perilous crossing to Europe. "The heartbreaking thing is that they believe Britain is a land of tolerance," he says. "They want to start their lives again, work and build a community - the things that we take for granted. They aren't looking for an easy ride, or to suck up bene-fits," he adds. "It's that connection that we'd like to make. Taking people to meet them might slowly change the prevailing, toxic attitude towards migrants as a threat, or sub-human."

On another occasion, Charles, who hosted Ukhip's first informal conference at his home in south-east London last night, helped talk a Syrian graphic designer out of setting off for England on a flimsy in-flatable raft in the middle of winter.

Since the closure of the Sangatte camp near Calais in 2002, migrants there have fended for themselves, camping in woods, dunes and abandoned buildings. Tensions have continued to rise among governments and anti-immigration groups on both sides of the Channel, only escalating earlier this year with the opening of a purpose-built camp outside the port.

Charles is no politician, but wants to promote empathy while a solution is sought. "The prank element of this is a way of getting attention but the real change happens when people say, maybe I'll go to Calais and make friends with people who have gambled their lives in the hope of achieving something approaching an acceptable level of human existence," he says.

Ukhip has raised just over £1,000 for Saturday's mission via its website (Ukhip.eu). Charles has had to scale back his flotilla plans and the group will stick to vans and cars on ferries. In Cornwall, meanwhile, Granville's granny is on board, too, collecting warm clothes and sleeping bags.

Simon Usborne

April 2015

JUST TRYING TO SURVIVE

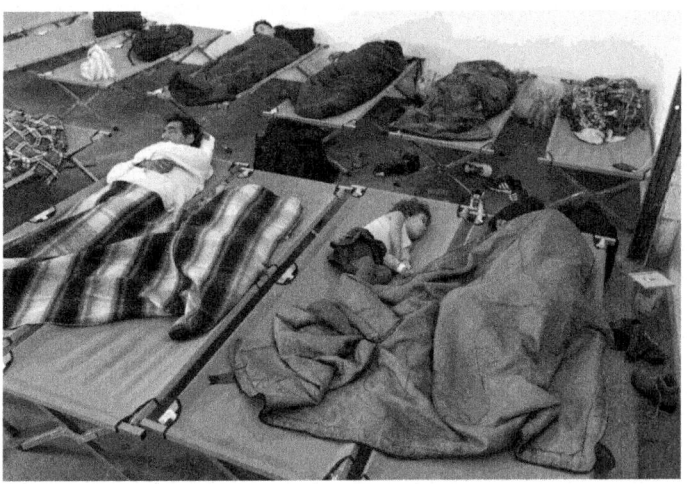

Refugees in Passau, Germany, 1 August 2015

6 April 2015

GATEWAY TO EUROPE

The occupants of the Amygdaleza Detention Centre in Athens are among about 3,500 detainees who will be released from the country's seven migrant camps if Greece's new anti-austerity rulers make good on their promises.

For people like Bilal Hussein it cannot come too soon. He was held in various detention centres in Greece, including Amygdaleza.

"It was horrible," he recalls. When the 34-year-old was released at the end of last month in the northern town of Xanthi, he was still wearing his summer clothes from the time he was arrested last year.

"It was cold but we had nothing to wear, only a T-shirt and trousers - not even socks."

He says he watched many inmates die from illnesses because of neglect and the lack of any healthcare at Amygdaleza.

"The [camp] was very dirty. If anyone got sick, no one cared - we'd get beaten up when we asked for a doctor," he tells i.

For years, Athens has repeatedly been condemned for its treatment of migrants by the European Court of Human Rights.

In its recently published report after visiting Amygdaleza in February, the non-governmental organisation Médecins du Monde (MDM) lamented the poor living conditions.

"It was really the image of a concentration camp," the head of Greece's branch of MDM, Nikitas Kanakis, said.

The left-wing Syriza party swept to power vowing to break with the policies of the past, and wants to free about 20 migrants every day, while ensuring the safe housing of 210 unaccompanied minors who are spread around the country's camps. It wants to shut the camps or transform them into open reception centres.

"There is a huge change in our government policy," Tasia Christodoulopoulou, the Immigration Minister, tells i.

But her opinion is not widely welcomed in a country that has become a main gateway into Europe for hundreds of thousands of migrants. The Athens mayor, George Kaminis, said: "We do not agree with this procedure, where hundreds of people are transported downtown [in Athens] without any concern about where they'll stay, eat, or survive."

Greece's stretched resources mean many refugees are denied their rights while the country is flooded with asylum-seekers it cannot handle.

But Greece's immigration policy is also being used by ministers as a pressure tool abroad. Due to its position on the south-eastern tip of Europe, one of the main points of entry for illegal immigration to the EU is Greece's border with Turkey - a country that jihadists travel through to enter the Isis territories of Iraq and Syria.

Last month, Panos Kammenos, junior coalition party leader and Defence Minister, told a meeting of his right-wing Independent Greeks party his government would suspend European treaties, allowing immigrants to move to the rest of the continent.

"If some have crossed to the side of Isis and that hasn't been checked, then the responsibility will lie with Europe," he warned.

Greece has one of the longest coastlines in Europe, making it an attractive option for illegal immigrants. Neighbouring Turkey has a huge refugee crisis from Syria.

Nathalie Savaricas

21 April 2015

TWISTED WORLD OF TRAFFICKING

The Omdurman market north of the Sudanese capital of Khartoum has been a thriving meeting place for sellers and buyers for centuries. Alongside the camels, leather and spices on offer is another much sought-after commodity these days - illegal passage from some of the world's poorest nations to Europe. The sprawling market is just one of dozens of way points that have sprung up across Africa to extract profit from the tide of humanity that flows out of countries from Eritrea and Syria to Ghana and Bangladesh in search of safety, a livelihood and a meaningful life.

In Omdurman, the people-smugglers do a lucrative trade in facilitating the travel of refugees from surrounding east African nations such as Eritrea, Ethiopia and Somalia into the Libyan desert region of Kufra and onwards to Tripoli where they await passage to the Italian island of Lampedusa and the "salvation" of Europe.

It is more than likely that among the 700 feared to have perished in a single night on board a fishing boat off Lampedusa in the early hours of Sunday, including many Eritreans, were several who had followed this route. Others will have come from different destinations - Egypt, West Africa and as far afield as Bangladesh.

According to the United Nations High Commissioner for Refugees, last year 219,000 people crossed the Mediterranean to Europe at a cost of 3,500 lives lost at sea. It is a growing tide - even before the improved weather brings a summer peak of migrants, some 31,000 made the journey in the first three months of this year with 1,500 deaths.

Nearly all will have paid a minimum of $2,000 (£1,340) - and many as much as $10,000 - to a global peoplesmuggling industry worth as much as $36bn a year.

According to UN figures, the largest contingents in the last two years have been those fleeing the civil war in Syria and one of the world's most repressive regimes in Eritrea. In July to September last year alone, some 6,000 Eritreans arrived on Italian shores after fleeing a country where arbitrary arrest and torture is endemic and military conscription is indefinite. The journey undertaken by these individuals from departure points stretching from Dhaka to Bamako - and converging more often than not on the Libyan coast - is about as long, exploited and treacherous as it is possible to find.

According to the Swissbased Global Initiative Against Transnational Organised Crime, each migrant will have paid a minimum of $2,000 for the land journey to reach the Libyan coast.

The most hazardous part of the journey to Europe is the final leg. The people-smugglers on the Libyan coast charge between $1,000 and $2,500 to reserve a place on their shoddy vessels for the 70-mile journey to Lampedusa. It is a grim industry where demand exceeds supply and the seller does not care greatly if the customer reaches their destination or not. Migrants are marshalled in villages under armed guard away from the coast and shown the boat to take them to Europe - all too often of far better quality than the one they will actually board. They are taken to the boats at night, herded into minibuses from which the seats have been ripped to maximise space.

Thereafter it is a Darwinian struggle for survival where money is the only currency and the smugglers maximise their profit by charging for "extras". A life jacket costs $200 and a place in the "firstclass" section of the boat - the top deck rather than being locked in the hull - is up to $300. In the twisted morality of this world, the traffickers think of everything. Pregnant women must pay $150 for the use of a catheter to counter the belief of some on board that the urine of a woman with child is poisonous.

Cahal Milmo

22 April 2015

GOLD MINE FOR TRAFFICKERS

Italian investigators have overheard leading organisers of the trade in people-trafficking mocking the dire predicament of refugees whose exploitation has made them millionaires.

The 34-year-old Eritrean, Mered Medhanie, known as "The General" and based in Tripoli, has boasted about the overcrowding of migrants on vessels that set off from the North African coast to Italy.

"They say I put too many aboard, but they're the ones who want to leave in a hurry," he said, laughing, according to reports of wiretap evidence in the Italian press yesterday. Prosecutors in Catania said yesterday that the Tunisian trafficker Mohammed Ali Malek, 27, arrested on suspicion of multiple manslaughter for causing last weekend's disaster in which 800 people died, had steered his crammed boat into a collision with a merchant ship, the King Jacob, that was coming to its rescue.

Another trafficker, Ermias Ghermay, said to have carved up much of the lucrative trade from Libya with Medhanie, was believed to be behind the tragedy in which 366 migrants drowned off the Italian island of Lampedusa in October 2013 - the disaster that forced the Italian government to introduce the Mare Nostrum search and-rescue mission. The Ethiopian migrant-turned-trafficker, declared last summer of some of his apparent paying customers: "They organised another trip a few days ago. I don't know what happened - they probably died."

Like Medhanie, Ghermay is living undisturbed in Tripoli, say Italian police. A wiretap ordered by Maurizio Scalia, deputy chief prosecutor in Palermo, Sicily, revealed Medhanie's indifference to the suffering.

"We do an illegal job - but what do you expect? We're not the government," he says, according to La Stampa newspaper, which quoted claims by law enforcement officials in Palermo that Ghermay's smuggling network had made €100m (£72m) in the past two years.

Police in Palermo, who on Monday arrested 15 people in an attempt to bust one of the Mediterranean's biggest people-smuggling rings, say the trafficking "Godfathers" are still at large in the Libyan capital.

The suspects were linked to the criminal organisation run by Ghermay.

Michael Day

25 April 2015

WAR, FAMINE, DROUGHT - THE UNHOLY TRINITY

For the last time: I agree with Nick. Earlier this week, the out-going Deputy Prime Minister at last backtracked on his government's part in the withdrawal last year of EU search-and rescue operations for migrants in the southern Mediterranean. Clegg argued that amid the proposals now aimed at stemming the flow, "It's all too easy to forget that they are human beings".

At the core of this mass quest for refuge lies not just a human body - like the 1,200, beyond Titanic's toll, drowned over the past week alone - but a human mind. That mind registers hardship and peril at home, chooses among options, gathers assets, plans a route, weighs the risks, and sets off on a journey into hope.

In the Mediterranean, we know how that journey has ended for 1,750 people already this year and about 3,300 last. However mis-guided, each of those shipwrecked (or, arguably, murdered) victims had taken a rational decision to flee conflict, penury or persecution - often enough, all three at once.

Forget the bloodless reckoning of "push factors" against "pull factors". From Syria to Nigeria, Iraq to Eritrea, every one of those lost souls who chose to entrust their fate to a frail craft on the Libyan shore run by a scheming crook will have acted from a wholly individual blend of hope and fear, aspiration and desperation.

Whichever course HMS Bulwark now plots (the Prime Minister promised the deployment of three naval vessels on Thursday), the people will still try to come. In 2014, 220,000 did make it across the Med to a mostly hostile Europe. The UK, for instance, has refused to match Germany and Sweden in offering some asylum places to Syrian refugees after a UN appeal for Europe to take in 130,000. And among the forces that conspire to uproot these ragged pilgrims lurk move-ments too profound for any fantasia of SAS strikes on smugglers' dens to eradicate. From Afghanistan to Nigeria, civil war, state breakdown and ethnic cleansing do wink on political radar screens. Further in the background, hard to isolate but even harder to mitigate, lies long-term climate change.

In yesterday's Chatham House speech on foreign policy, instantly spun as an assault on David Cameron over post-conflict drift in Libya, Ed Miliband did in fact make the faintest of nods towards the deeper drivers of global turmoil. He said that "what we have seen in Libya is that when tensions over power and resource began to emerge, they simply reinforced deep-seated ideological and ethnic fault lines in the country".

Those "resource" tensions will shake and scar an increasingly thirsty and crowded planet long after every current political career has closed. In bits and pieces, evidence for the links between political instability, mass migration and environmental crisis has mounted for more than a decade. In March, these once-speculative debates reached some front pages. A US study in the Proceedings of the National Academy of Sciences connected the unprecedented stretch of drought in Syria between 2006 and 2010 to rural depopulation, an upsurge of social and sectarian unrest in fast-expanding cities, and the outbreak of revolt against Bashar al-Assad.

Correlation is not causation. In sites of upheaval, the roots of conflict may knit together beyond all disentanglement. All the same, as the co-author of the Syrian study Richard Seager phrased it: "A drought made worse by climate change was one important factor that initiated the social unravelling." In Iraq, according to meteorologist Eric Holthaus, the sudden ascent of Isis partnered record seasons of heat. Holthaus quotes Frank Femia of the Washington think-tank the Center for Climate and Security: "You can't say climate change is causing Isis to do what it's doing, but it certainly has a role to play in the region."

In 2009, research found a correlation in sub-Saharan Africa between rising average temperatures and the likelihood of civil strife. To the US Defence Department, climate change ranks as a "threat multiplier". Hillary Clinton, as Secretary of State, commissioned an intelligence report that foresaw "water wars" breaking out from 2022 as aquifers dried, lakes and rivers parched and rains failed.

In East Africa, a pact last month between Egypt and Ethiopia has for the moment silenced the mutual threats that arose from the latter's $5bn plan to harvest the Blue Nile via the - already half-built - "Grand Ethiopian Renaissance Dam". In 2012, Michael Werz of the Center for American Progress studied the role played by environmental stress in migration across northwest Africa. This week, writing for Reuters with Max Hoffman, he reiterated that "climate and demographic trends can squeeze the margins of life at the family and community levels, contribute to decisions to migrate, heighten conflicts over basic resources and threaten state structures and regional stability".

At the southern end of trans-Saharan routes towards the sea and Europe, Nigeria - now scourged by the insurgency of Boko Haram - annually loses more than 1,350 square miles of land to desertification. Its population will double by 2040. Lake Chad - which sustains 25 million people - has lost 95 per cent of its volume since 1960. "Nobody would argue that climate change is the only factor," warn Werz and Hoffman. However, "the second-order effects of climate change - undermined agriculture and competition for water and food resources - can contribute to instability and to higher numbers of migrants".

The hunt for a single overarching cause behind the great shifts in history has a long and questionable pedigree. Neither lead poisoning nor homosexuality caused the downfall of the Roman Empire, as crackpots used to claim. Less fancifully, attendance at a Protestant church did not by itself transform northern Europeans into profit-hungry capitalists. Plausible pictures of seismic change take the form of clusters rather than chains. Yet a scientific weather eye, sharpened by new ways of decoding data, can now spot patterns in what contemporaries saw as discrete disasters.

In his 2013 book Global Crisis, Yale historian Geoffrey Parker looks to the cooling of the "Little Ice Age", with its sodden summers, ruined harvests and deep-frozen winters, as a partial explanation for the catastrophic wars, famines and rebellions that convulsed the mid-17th century. This chill wind toppled thrones and smashed societies from India to Spain, China to Germany. So did Charles I lose his head in January 1649 because of climate change? Not exclusively, of course. Still, such a perspective may widen the ripples of our understanding.

The problem with such a supersized interpretation is that it may leave us feeling even more helpless than before, paralysed into inertia by the daunting scale of forces now at work. At Durham University, David Held - master of University College and professor of politics and international relations - is a keynote speaker at a conference in June on human migration and the environment. Using the now-popular term for the epoch of man-made environmental change coined by chemist Paul Crutzen, it will ask: "How should we conceive of migration in the Anthropocene?"

However, the advent of the "Anthropocene" alone has not shattered Syria, Iraq and Libya. A harsh critic of the "9/11 wars" and their chaotic aftermaths, Professor Held underlines that the wreckage left by botched Western interventions has done more than enough to leave Libya an anarchic mess where human smugglers flourish. The ousting of Gaddafi without any plan B has left "a catastrophe that has destabilised the region from Mali to Tunisia", he says.

"The breakdown of the Libyan state has created a pathway and provided an impetus for people to move in increasing numbers," Professor Held argues. At the same time, leaders in the intended destinations drag their feet and wring their hands. "The EU is at its most fragile for the past 20 years. The 1990s model of Europe as the great soft power, against the hard power of the US, is much diminished." Whatever combination of warfare, weather and dreams of betterment may drive them, survivors of the passage land in a weakened bloc. It responds to calamity late, or not at all. "Solidarity," Professor Held notes, "rarely grows under conditions of economic insecurity."The EU "wants to present a cosmopolitan external face but at the same time, internally, it's a battleground for major states".

With those states' governments in thrall at home to right-wing isolationists, the EU has held out the prospect of a meagre 5,000 places for the most vulnerable refugees from ethnic cleansing and civil war. Too little, too late? It always is. Yet even tokens matter. If you wish to put a human face to the desperate quest for asylum, visit Liverpool Street station in London. There, on "Hope Square", stand the five bronze children of Frank Meisler and Arie Ovadia's statue The Arrival. They commemorate that Kindertransport that, from 1938 to 1940, brought 10,000 unaccompanied young refugees (including Meisler himself) out of peril in Hitler's Europe. As a gesture of humanity in another frightened time, it was not remotely enough, but it was not nothing.

Contemplate these ageless kids - one with a teddy bear, another with a violin - and you see them gaze towards a future that despite all pain and loss feels ripe with possibility. Above all, read the lines from the Talmud inscribed beside the group: "Whosoever rescues a single soul is credited as though they had saved the whole world."

Boyd Tonkin

May 2015

GRASPING FOR A SOLUTION

HMS Bulwark, 28 May 2013

11 May 2015

GUNBOAT DIPLOMACY PROPOSED

Their deaths have appalled the world. In record numbers, would-be migrants have perished at sea attempting to escape the chaos of their homelands for the safety of Europe. As the crisis has grown, so have calls for action.

Today, the European Union unveils its response: gunboat diplomacy. The EU will seek United Nations backing for a plan to seek and destroy the boats used by people traffickers to ferry migrants from the Libyan coast to the shores of Europe. The plan is likely to face tricky questions over its mandate in Libyan waters, while aid agencies say it will do nothing to stop the crisis.

The proposal to send gunships into Libya's territorial waters will be presented to the UN Security Council in New York by EU foreign policy supremo Federica Mogherini.

France, Britain, Spain and Lithuania (the EU members on the 15-nation Security Council) have drafted a resolution seeking authority for the use of force.

The draft calls for the "use of all means to destroy the business model of the traffickers", in international high seas. The text rules out the destruction of boats while they are in Libya's territorial waters or of vessels sailing under international flags, but it does seek permission to seize vessels in high seas, as well as Libyan territorial waters and Libyan coast before they embark with migrants.

The plan says vessels such as the Royal Navy flagship HMS Bulwark would be stationed in Libyan waters, while helicopter gunships would be dispatched to "neutralise" the ships used by traffickers. Italy, the main landing point for the migrants, would take operational command of the mission, which has already secured commitments from 10 EU member states, including Britain, France and Spain.

Libya is now the main launching point for sea-crossings to Europe: the country's descent into factional fighting has effectively left it lawless, with a vacuum of authority. Last month as many as 950 people died in a single incident when the boat they were travelling in capsized off the coast of Italy.

However, UN approval for the EU plan is far from certain. Ms Mogherini, who visited Beijing last week, is confident that China will not wield its veto. But although her entourage and the Italian government say Russia is ready to co-operate, there are doubts whether Moscow - still embroiled in a tense diplomatic standoff with the EU over Ukraine - can be won round. Libya's UN ambassador, Ibrahim Dabbashi, opposes the EU mission. He says the best deal for Europe to address the crisis is to give his Western-backed government arms to help fight the rival government backed by Islamist militias.

Meanwhile, the militia that controls Libya's coastal capital, Tripoli, has promised to "confront" any EU moves.

UN Secretary General Ban Ki-moon has added to the criticism, saying there could be "no military solution" to the migrants crossing the Mediterranean.

Aid agencies have warned that the plans would do nothing to stop the underlying refugee crisis. "We must find a more comprehensive solution than just bombing bases and these little boats," said Francesco Rocca, who heads the Red Cross in Italy.

EU leaders agreed action last month to "identify, capture and destroy vessels before they are used by traffickers". Many refugees are fleeing violence in Syria and Libya, but others have come from conflict-ridden countries as far away as Somalia, Nigeria and Congo.

The military plans will also be discussed by EU foreign ministers meeting this week, and then by EU leaders at a summit next month.

They will be complemented by a broad European Agenda on Migration, which the European Commission is set to adopt on Wednesday. The five-year programme aims to address asylum, trafficking, irregular migration, external borders and legal migration in a single package.

While the naval mission will grab the headlines, the commission says its initiative deals with some of the more thorny issues about immigration that many member states have skated over. These include the underlying questions about why migrants come to Europe; how many are needed to keep the economy ticking; how many will public opinion accept; and what measures would be needed to control the flow, other than destroying the boats.

The aim is a quota system to spread migrants more evenly across the EU. This would both ease the burden on Italy and other members states in the south, but also help countries such as Germany and Sweden, which between them end up with almost half of the EU's asylumseekers. "The EU needs a permanent system for sharing the responsibility for large numbers of refugees and asylum seekers among member states," the draft commission text says.

Hungarian Prime Minister Viktor Orban, who leads the right-wing Fidesz party, has already lambasted the commission proposals, saying last Friday: "The European concept of someone letting immigrants into their country and then distributing them among the other member states is a mad and unfair idea."

Nearly 63,500 migrants have arrived in Europe this year, according to the International Organisation for Migration (IOM). Nearly 2,000 have perished in the sea crossings, almost 10 times the number of deaths from the same period last year.

Leo Cendrowicz

19 May 2015

GUNBOAT DIPLOMACY ACCEPTED

European warships could be dispatched to the Mediterranean "within weeks" to seize and sink boats used by people smugglers in Libya under a military plan agreed by European Union foreign and defence ministers in Brussels last night.

The mission is part of the EU's response to the recent surge of migrants crossing the Mediterranean to reach Europe. However, plans to intercept the traffickers' boats could be delayed or even blocked if the EU does not secure a mandate from the UN Security Council and support from the conflicting authorities in Libya. EU foreign policy chief Federica Mogherini said that if enough military pledges are made, the mission could be fully launched by the time EU leaders meet at their summit on 25 June. "This is just the beginning. The operational planning starts, the force generation starts," Ms Mogherini said.

The first phase of the operation, which does not need UN approval, involves setting up a system to exchange classified intelligence and data on the smuggling rings.

The naval mission already has received pledges of warships from Britain, France, Germany, Italy and Spain. The United Nations says some 60,000 people have tried to make the perilous crossing this year, with around 1,800 migrants dying. The mission, called EU Navfor Med, will be run from Rome.

In parallel, officials will work on the UN Security Council resolution needed for the third phase of the plan, to seize and destroy the boats not only in international high seas, but in Libya's territorial waters. Officials admit if ships have a national flag, they can only be seized with consent of the flag state - although they can be boarded and searched without the state's permission. "After we take the decision it is more likely for the Security Council to take a resolution," Ms Mogherini said.

She underlined that sinking migrant smuggler boats was a means to an end, which was the destruction of the smuggler networks. "The fundamental point is not the destruction of the vessels but of the business models," she said. Nato secretary general Jens Stoltenberg told ministers that Islamic extremists could try hiding amongst the migrants heading for Europe. "There might be foreign fighters, there might be terrorists trying to hide," he said.

Amnesty International has warned that armed action could force migrants trapped in Libya into making dangerous crossings anyway. "Focusing on combating transnational organised crime and smuggling without allowing thousands of migrants and refugees to access a place of safety would be grossly inadequate," John Dalhuisen, Amnesty International's Director for Europe and Central Asia said.

The United Nations High Commissioner for Refugees (UNHCR) is also concerned about whether the EU would be able to ensure refugees and asylum-seekers are not casualties. The decision on the military mission came amid uncertainty about a broader EU response to the migrant crisis, with France and Spain now joining Britain in opposing proposals from the European Commission for quotas to relocate migrants around Europe.

Leo Cendrowicz

25 May 2015

THE WEST HELPED CREATE THE PLIGHT OF MIGRANTS

On Question Time, an Asian man slams the Government for failing to stem migration, and damns migrants as "benefits tourists".

He speaks broken English and is clearly a migrant himself. Yet he smears all recent incomers and presumes to know their motives for trying to enter Britain.

Education Secretary Nicky Morgan, one of the panellists in last week's edition of the programme, does the same.

Meanwhile, David Cameron tries to explain the latest immigration figures - the highest for a decade. He impugns Vince Cable and the

Liberal Democrats, accuses people-traffickers and migrants themselves.

These are now the established, unopposed narratives. After years of ferocious migrantbashing, the national psyche has been successfully reprogrammed: millions of our citizens truly believe that humans from the old Soviet Union, Africa, Asia and the Middle East are flocking to get at those gorgeous council flats and big, fat, state handouts.

So easy isn't it? Just blame those who can't answer back. Don't think too deeply about why there is this movement of peoples and how they feel before, during and after they leave their homelands.

The Battersea Arts Centre is currently showcasing The Siege, a raw, theatrical enactment of tense months in 2002 when the Israeli army besieged the Church of the Nativity in Bethlehem. The church had given sanctuary to Palestinian fighters.

In the end, a deal was negotiated by European Union leaders. The Israelis pulled back and the Palestinians were sent into permanent exile. The most moving moment comes when they talk about banishment. They live in the West, have security and life chances. But the aching pain of displacement goes on and they cannot be happy.

Most migrants carry that sense of loss, even those who went off voluntarily to seek better fortune. Those who have never felt the need or pressure to emigrate can't empathise with them, for that would be a chink in their fortress mentality. Fear is a terrible thing. It depletes compassion.

To many Britons, the current crisis is disconnected from history, and from global geopolitics. Again, it is so much easier to think of "them" and "us", and disregard Western culpabilities, past and present.

In 2011, David Cameron, on a visit to Pakistan, accepted that Britain was responsible for many of the world's intractable problems. It was the first and only time I recall a British leader accepting that colonialism left fractures and stains which have led to discord and failed states. (Margaret Thatcher, as well as Tony Blair and Gordon Brown, extolled the Empire and the subjugation of millions.) Mr Cameron was savaged by the right-wing press and Labour's Tristram Hunt. Maybe that is why he never again spoke candidly about that history. Silence is the path of least resistance.

No, you can't just blame white people for post-colonial chaos and failures. Since independence, leaders have almost all been incompetent, corrupt and callous. Dictatorships and one-party rule, profligacy and greed, have despoiled potentially productive nations, turning them into hopeless, dependent, unsustainable entities. But the case against old European imperialists is strong and indubitable.

Last week, one Drusilla Long had a letter in a newspaper about desperate and desperately unwanted migrants. She was raised in Ghana during British rule. "I believe [we should] return some of the immense wealth we all stole from these countries, such as gold, diamonds, etc, which we have long used to build up our own wealthy 'fortress' Europe," she wrote.

Brave woman, saying the unsayable. Then there is the continuing support this country gives to oppressive regimes, the arms we sell, and the wars we have launched in the past 20 years. Iraqis never chose to become resented refugees, nor did Afghans.

Libya is now the export depot for hungry, frightened, distressed people. The allies who bombed the place have gone and feel no obligation for the mess they left. Many Isis insurgents are from Saddam Hussein's old Baathist army. True, we did not intervene in Syria, but for decades Bashar al-Assad was propped up by us, as was his equally heinous father. Many of the migrants trying to get into Europe come from these places. They are hated perhaps because they remind us of our bad policies and actions. Are these then our noble British values? When bigots tell me to go back to where I came from, I remind them I am here because the British government supported Idi Amin's bid for power. A million or more black Ugandans fled or were killed. Some fled to the UK. Has Britain ever admitted this was a big mistake? (Don't, please, fire off letters accusing me of hating this country. Fair criticism is not hatred.) Among the flotsam and jetsam of wandering humans are "economic migrants" who are seen as the biggest threat of all. They, too, are victims of Western games and unending austerity measures. We know how that affects the vulnerable and should understand why people die trying to escape poverty.

The International Monetary Fund (IMF) and World Bank have driven down spending on health and education across Africa and elsewhere. Developing world debt is used by the West to cut the cost of raw materials and steal resources. Privatisation is the condition for borrowing money. It stinks.

Anup Shah is the editor of the excellent www.globalissues.org. He writes about the unjust trading system. The West protects its interests and pushes poorer countries to supply materials, labour and goods at the lowest costs. To be a dumping ground, too.

The EU, IMF and World Bank must transform the system; our leaders need to tell more truths about the dispossessed. Xenophobia, withdrawal of welfare and gunboats won't stop the tide of humanity coming to our shores. They come because they have no choice. But the West does.

Yasmin Alibhai-Brown

28 May 2015

RELOCATION PLAN

The European Commission said it would pay EU member states up to €6,000 (£4,250) for each refugee taken as part of a plan to accept 40,000 asylum seekers from Syria and Eritrea over the next two years, yesterday.

The proposed payments, for relocation and housing, are the latest EU response to the migration crisis that has seen more than 80,000 people crossing the Mediterranean to Europe so far this year, and over 1,800 perishing on the journey.

The plan details how the 40,000 asylum-seekers will be spread across Europe, with Germany (21.91 per cent), France (16.88) and Spain (10.72) assigned the biggest quotas. "This is a fair distribution," EU Home Affairs Commissioner Dimitris Avramopoulos said in Brussels. He pleaded for "minimum solidarity" for Italy and Greece, the main gateway states for the migrants.

In return, Italy and Greece will have step up efforts to properly identify and fingerprint each asylum seeker upon arrival - they would then be relocated to another member state or sent back to their home country.

However, the €240 million (£170m) plans are likely to run into fierce opposition, with many EU governments already baulking at the idea of quotas. France, initially a supporter of the scheme, is now vociferously opposed to quotas. Spain, Hungary, Slovakia and Estonia have also raised concerns, while Britain, Ireland and Denmark - who have the right not to take part - all say they will opt out of the scheme.

Commission President Jean-Claude Juncker acknowledged this reticence, while urging EU governments to go do more to address the crisis. "It would seem that some member states are reluctant, but they have to accept that it's not about words, it's about action," Juncker said.

The relocation plan was backed by United Nations Secretary General Ban Ki-moon. But Mr Ban was cautious about another element of the EU's reponse, a proposed naval mission agreed by foreign ministers last week to stop peoplesmuggling gangs operating in the Mediterranean. "Our priority should be given to life saving," he said.

Leo Cendrowicz

June 2015

THOUSANDS FLEEING

Refugees arrive on inflatable dinghy, Lesvos, Greece, 12 October 2015

8 June 2015

'THE ROYAL NAVY HAS SAVED MY LIFE'

A British warship rescued more than 1,000 desperate migrants making the perilous journey from Libya to Italy yesterday, in the Royal Navy's biggest Mediterranean rescue mission.

Royal Marine Commandos scrambled to help children as young as two and heavily pregnant women on to HMS Bulwark, which had been dispatched to the region as the UK's contribution to the international response to the migrant crisis.

Last night, one woman was in labour after her waters broke on a dinghy shortly before she was rescued just 20 miles off the coast of Libya.

She joined hundreds of others, including Syrians, Africans and Pakistanis, who were piled into the lower deck of the Royal Navy ship after the extraordinary operation beginning at 5.50am. Others had to be taken on to the upper deck and were set to spend the night outside due to lack of space.

As the sun set on the British ship, around 1,100 migrants had been rescued from nine heavily overcrowded boats.

Asha Kulubari, 26, had travelled from Bamako, Mali, with her husband, and her child Fatima. "I'm so happy to be saved," she said. "I'm so happy these men saved us. I have my baby and nothing else."

Those rescued yesterday had travelled for as long as 10 hours from various towns and beaches across the Libyan coast. Some described the journey as a living hell. Yasin, 29, from Islamabad, Pakistan, said: "The Royal Navy has saved my life."

Some of those rescued were carrying €50 notes hidden in small plastic bags, while many of them had nothing after they said the people-traffickers had taken everything.

One woman, who was four months' pregnant, said she had made the "terrifying" journey with her husband to escape terrorism.

Rose, 21, from Nigeria, said she wanted to go anywhere: "Germany, Britain, any place. Any place which will give me and my husband the papers."

Rose, who paid $1,200 (£800) to get on the ship, said: "We left our three-yearold daughter back home with my mother-in-law to look after her because we didn't have the money to bring her with us.

"It was truly terrifying, I was very sick on that wooden boat and was vomiting all the time. Back home there was much danger so that is why we made this journey. I was very scared for my baby but now these people have saved us and I feel very safe and very happy. We want our daughter to come too one day."

Another migrant had asked: "How long will it take to get to London?" Yesterday was the busiest day for HMS Bulwark since it was deployed to the Mediterranean last month, as large numbers of migrants travelled from the city of Zawarah, Libya, to take advantage of calm seas.

Eight inflatable dinghies, described as "lilos with sides", and one huge wooden boat were spotted by radar and the ship's two Merlin helicopters. Each operation involved drawing up two assault boats each side of the migrant vessel so that the passengers would not surge to one side and capsize the crowded boat.

After receiving water and life jackets they were then guided by the Marines on to larger craft usually used for sea-to-land assaults.

A Pakistani man in his forties told Royal Marines searching him that he had been stabbed and shot in Libya. "Last night we were beaten and threatened and were in a camp for three days, sometimes they gave us water but no food," he said.

"On board the boat I was very frightened, it was especially bad for the women, they treated us like sheep, like goats. I brought my own water when I got on the boat, they took it off me. It was very bad, people were suffocating and there was crying, and one or two fainted."

The rescued migrants are now likely to be taken to Sicily where they will be able to register as asylum-seekers or make their way to other European countries, including Britain.

It was truly terrifying but in Nigeria there is much danger.

Larisa Brown

9 June 2015

LIKE 'A BOMB READY TO EXPLODE' IN ITALY

The arrival of thousands more migrants in southern Italy at the weekend has reignited the row between Rome and the northern regions, with one centre-right leader saying the migrant crisis was "a bomb ready to explode".

More than 5,800 migrants were saved from the Mediterranean at the weekend, including 1,200 people rescued by the Royal Navy off the coast of Libya.

But with Italy's interior ministry indicating that many of the new arrivals would be sent to northern regions such as Lombardy, Veneto and Piedmonte, and press reports that coaches were being readied to transfer over 3,000 migrants, right-wing politicians reacted angrily yesterday.

Roberto Maroni, the governor of Italy's most populous region, Lombardy, and a senior figure in the anti-immigration Northern League, has threatened to withhold funds from municipalities in his region that accepted more migrants from Sicily.

Piero Fassino, the left-wing mayor of Turin, in neighbouring Piedmonte, said such action would be illegal.

Mr Maroni was backed, however, by Luca Zaia, the Northern League governor of Veneto, who said that his region was unable to house more migrants. Veneto was, he said, "like a bomb ready to explode". The centre-right governor of Liguria, Giovanni Toti, also said his region would not take any more refugees.

The Prime Minister, Matteo Renzi, hit back at Mr Maroni, saying it was no good for Italy to call on the rest of Europe to help it bear the burden of the migrant crisis when parts of Italy were acting so selfishly.

"Enough posturing, I'd call on everyone, including northern governors, to rediscover a bit of common sense," he said. Mr Renzi had said in a TV interview on Sunday that he considered the EU's response to the migrant crisis "largely insufficient".

More than 50,000 migrants fleeing poverty and war in Africa and the Middle East have arrived in Italy by boat since the start of the year. Around 20,000 asylum-seekers are due to be resettled in other EU nations.

Corriere Della Sera reported that the interior ministry was ready to start using army barracks to house the arrivals. Meanwhile, a United Nations report has warned that Eritrea's government may have committed crimes against humanity. "It is not law that rules Eritreans - but fear," said the report, which detailed extrajudicial killings, sexual slavery and enforced labour.

The situation has prompted hundreds of thousands of people to flee the country, according to UN investigators. Eritrean military conscription for 18-year-olds is thought to have added to the exodus.

Michael Day

17 June 2015

ANGRY WAR OF WORDS WITHIN THE EU

As Italy threatened to let tens of thousands of migrants loose across the European Union, interior ministers attempted yesterday to hammer out a compromise deal to tackle the growing refugee crisis, agreeing a plan for EU-managed "hotspots" in Italy and Greece where migrants would be held and processed.

European officials would make sure migrants were finger-printed, with asylum seekers sorted from illegal economic migrants. "Those who have no right to stay must be returned to their home country, and we agree that returns should increasingly be dealt by at EU level," said Italy's Interior Minister, Angelino Alfano.

The outline deal, which contained few specifics and did not spell out how illegal migrants would be sent home, followed an increasingly angry war of words that set Italy at loggerheads with its European neighbours, particularly France. After French authorities drafted in ranks of police to prevent migrants from Italy crossing the border at Ventimiglia, Italian police were forced to round up crowds of unwilling men, women and children and push them on to buses to remove them from the border area - providing unedifying images as the emergency summit opened in Luxembourg.

As he arrived, Mr Alfano accused France of flouting Schengen open-border rules and called its stance at Ventimiglia a "punch in the face for Europe". He added: "Everyone should learn what's happening from the scenes at Ventimiglia. It's a punch in the eye to those who want to look the other way."

Hundreds of migrants from the Horn of Africa had been huddled on rocks by the sea, wrapped in foil, before they were put on buses and returned to the railway station.

Meanwhile, some residents of the Italian border town have begun driving migrants across the passport-free French border by car, for fees of €70 a head. Local police estimated that 150 a day have been slipping through this way.

Mr Alfano's French counterpart, Bernard Cazeneuve, denied that France had closed its border at Ventimiglia. "When migrants cross borders and it is established that they arrived in Italy, then it is only normal that they return to Italy," he said, adding that French border police were allowed to check documents.

France and Germany proposed what they called a "compromise" deal on how to distribute asylum seekers around the EU. German Interior Minister Thomas de Maiziere said: "There won't be a result on this, but there might be a corridor leading to a compromise."

But doubts remained over whether all EU countries would accept quotas. Earlier proposals to redistribute across the EU the 24,000 asylum seekers currently in Italy and 16,000 in Greece appear to have collapsed as one EU member after another backed away from the plan.

The UK has said in no uncertain terms that it will not accept migrant quotas from southern Europe. Britain's Home Secretary, Theresa May, who attended the meeting with her European counterparts, instead called for action to tackle the human traffickers who brought migrants to Europe on rickety boats.

The migrant crisis in the Mediterranean was "reaching our borders", she said, and "putting great pressure" on European towns and cities. "To deal with this issue in the long term we need to go after the criminal gangs who are plying a terrible, callous trade in human lives," she added.

Save The Children has stepped up the pressure on the UK by calling for Britain to agree to take in 1,500 unaccompanied youngsters who had made the crossing to Europe.

If Italy fails to get what it considers to be sufficient support, Prime Minister Matteo Renzi has said he will take unilateral action under an asyet undefined "plan B". One option would be for asylum seekers in Italy to receive three-month residence passes that would allow them to travel around most of the EU, enabling them to head towards northern Europe.

But Mr Renzi is also thought to be considering get-out clauses in the 2003 Dublin agreement under which asylum applicants must remain within the EU state where they first register, which in practice limits thousands to staying in Italy and Greece.

Some observers say Article 17 of the agreement could be invoked, which would allow member states to "waive such responsibility for humanitarian and compassionate reasons". This could mean refugees being allowed to leave Italy to join family already inside other EU countries.

Franco Miranelli, a senator in Mr Renzi's Democratic Party, said the Italian Prime Minister would have to continue the tough talking at next week's full summit of EU leaders. Mr Renzi is also expected to press the issue when he meets David Camerom in Milan today.

Sources at the interior ministry said officials were considering whether to stop allowing migrants rescued from non-Italian vessels to disembark on Italian soil. This was backed by right-wing parliamentarians. Maurizio Gasparri, the deputy speaker of the Senate, said on Tuesday morning: "Last week the British [Navy] rescued hundreds of migrants and brought them to Italy. Great, you did well, but why not take them to the UK and do your part, too?" Such a move might hasten the departure of HMS Bulwark, which is due to end its role helping to rescue migrants crossing the Mediterranean within three weeks.

In Bolzano, where hundreds of migrants are trapped near the Austrian border, the police chief Lucio Carluccio called for the rest of Italy to adopt its methods. He said the small provincial capital was at least providing food, clothing, medical care and accommodation for those massed in its railways stations.

Michael Day

17 June 2015

'SEEK GOD'S FORGIVENESS IF YOU REFUSE MIGRANTS'

The Pope heaped pressure on David Cameron today to reconsider Britain's refusal to accept migrants rescued from the Mediterranean by criticising nations who "close the door" to them.

Pope Francis also suggested that "people and institutions" who shut the door to the migrants should seek forgiveness from God.

His intervention came just hours before the Prime Minister met Italian Prime Minister Matteo Renzi in Milan for talks on the Mediterranean crisis.

"I invite you all to ask forgiveness for the persons and the institutions who close the door to these people who are seeking a family, who are seeking to be protected," the Pope said at the end of his weekly general audience. Italy is threatening to give migrants papers to allow them to move across the Schengen borderless EU area.

It has also threatened to restrict the Royal Navy disembarking rescued people at its ports unless other European nations agree to take their "share" of 40,000 migrants who have made it across the Mediterranean.

Standing in for Mr Cameron at Prime Minister's Questions, Chancellor George Osborne stressed that the UK is a humanitarian nation and would continue to be part of the maritime rescue operation even if HMS Bulwark is withdrawn for refitting. But he added that key to solving the crisis was "breaking the link" which attracted growing numbers of people in northern Africa to cram into boats and set off across the Mediterranean in search of a better life in Europe.

France and Austria have stepped up border controls on migrants coming from Italy, turning back hundreds and leaving growing numbers camped out in railway stations in Rome and Milan.

Experts expect the numbers of migrants to increase, with a significant number of them heading to Britain.

Nicholas Cecil

21 June 2015

'WE DON'T FEEL LIKE WE'RE HUMAN HERE'

The overcrowded makeshift camp, lacking bathrooms, food and blankets, is not how the refugees imagined Europe. But Greece is struggling to cope with the tide of boats arriving on its islands from neighbouring Turkey. Amid an economic crisis, the country has received more than 55,000 refugees since January, an almost tenfold increase on the 6,500 arrivals in the first five months of last year.

Lesvos, an island just five miles from the Turkish coast, has been bearing the brunt of the influx. More than 20,000 refugees - from Afghanistan, Syria, Libya and elsewhere - have arrived on its shores this year. With the peak season for migration set to begin, the island is already overwhelmed. Some 3,000 refugees are currently on Lesvos, according to the UN refugee agency UNHCR.

The island's reception camp, close to the capital, Mytilene, has a capacity of 400 but now shelters more than 1,000 refugees waiting for the papers that will allow them to continue on to Athens.

Last month, the municipality opened an emergency camp in nearby Karatepe. It is already overcrowded. Last week, hundreds of refugees marched to the port of Mytilene, protesting against the living conditions in the camp. In Karatepe, 1,000 refugees share two toilets, one each for men and women. A hose serves as a shower. Some sleep under tarpaulin sheets, others in flimsy camping tents.

"We sleep on the floor without blankets. It's cold at night and it's dirty. It's full of mosquitoes," said a 15-year-old refugee from Kabul who arrived in Lesvos last weekend. She asked for her name to be withheld for fear of endangering her registration process. "It's terrible here. The toilets are so dirty, they don't have doors, and I don't think it's safe here for women," she added. "My father has asthma and he can't get a spray. If I ask the guards something, they shout at us."

For two days, she and her family stayed in Moria, the main reception camp, before being transferred to Karatepe on Monday. In Moria, conditions were better, she said.

She was told her papers would take another 10 days. Refugees arriving on Greek islands have to wait for registration in order to board a ship to Athens, but the surge in arrivals has created a backlog, putting a considerable strain on the island's facilities. Public sector cuts have left local authorities understaffed and without enough funding to deal with the crisis.

The Mayor of Lesvos, Spyros Galinos, has appealed for help, describing the situation as "unmanageable".

"People are running out of resources," said William Spindler, a UNHCR spokesman who visited Lesvos recently. "They're barely coping - you could say that they're not really coping. The quantity and quality of the food aren't very good. There's not enough space for all of them. The conditions are very bad," he told The Independent on Sunday.

Last Wednesday, lunch for the refugees at Karatepe was a single supermarket croissant. Refugees said that on previous days they had been given biscuits. Many find themselves unable to observe Ramadan, which began last week, as, without enough food to eat at night, they cannot fast in the day.

UNHCR, which has two staff members on the island, has distributed basic supplies to the most needy but, overall, Lesvos receives little outside support. While Médecins du Monde and METAction, a Greek NGO, work in the main camp of Moria, the rudimentary camp in Karatepe has been left under the supervision of a small number of coastguards.

Overseeing the food distribution, one threw her hands in the air: "There are a thousand people here. There are no doctors. We really need doctors here," she said.

If the southern region around Mytilene gets little support, the north of Lesvos, which is closest to Turkey, receives none. Locals have stepped in to provide food and shelter for the refugees.

In the small town of Eftalou, Eric Kempson, a British artist who has lived on Lesvos for 16 years, gets up at 5am every morning to scour the sea for arriving boats. When they come ashore, he and his family bring them food, water and blankets, and provide first aid to the injured.

"We've gotten no help from aid agencies, not in the north. We've had to sleep up to 200 people sometimes at the bus stop, for three or four days, and we've had to feed them, with more coming in," he said. "We need aid agencies. We're just people. We need a doctor here; we need resources. I don't know why they haven't come up here, we've been screaming for months."

When refugees arrive in the north of the island, they face a long walk to the camps. As Greek legislation bans buses, taxis and other drivers from taking undocumented migrants in their vehicles, the 70km road from the northern port town of Molyvos to Mytilene is lined with men, women and children making their way south. "We walked for two days after arriving in Greece, only to find this," said Ahmad Wali, an Afghan refugee sharing a tiny camping tent in Karatepe with his wife and three children. A former USAID driver in Kandahar, Wali made the journey to Europe after receiving threats for having worked with Americans. He was clutching a letter that recommended his immediate evacuation, which was never carried out.

Another refugee, Ahmed, 21, arrived last Sunday, fleeing military conscription in Syria. Having been told by coastguards in Mytilene that there was not enough space in the camp, he and his friends were preparing to sleep in a nearby park.

"I didn't think it would be like this," he said, his fellow refugees nodding. "I thought we would feel human in Europe. We don't feel like we're human here."

Zia Weise

July 2015

CALAIS AGAIN

Boundry of ferry terminal, Calais, France

29 July 2015

CHANNEL TUNNEL A MAJOR POLITICAL HEADACHE

Today's meeting of the Government's Cobra emergency committee on the Channel Tunnel crisis is stark confirmation that what started as a human tragedy has also become a major political headache.

The trouble for Theresa May, normally so effective at dealing with problems on her watch, is that most of the solutions to the worsening situation lie outside her control.

The promise of more money for fencing, detection equipment and sniffer dogs will help hard-pressed Eurotunnel staff and British border guards stop at least some migrants hiding in UKbound lorries and trains.

But with thousands camped in Calais, making daily attempts to reach this country, and vast flows of refugees across the Mediterranean continuing, such measures amount to little more than sticking plasters on a gaping wound.

More effective treatment is needed. To begin with, the French authorities could do a better job of protecting the tunnel and the roads leading up to it. Clearing migrant camps would help too.

So would ensuring that other European countries, including France, fulfil their obligations under the EU's Dublin Regulation. It stipulates that asylum claims should be dealt with in the first safe country reached by a migrant.

Failure in these areas has allowed the problem in Calais to spiral, now almost out of control, with the numbers seeking to breach the Channel Tunnel defences rocketing in response.

Migration further afield, notably across the Mediterranean from Africa, but also from Afghanistan and the east, is the biggest challenge.

Mrs May hopes to persuade France and other EU countries to repatriate more of these migrants to deter even greater flows in the future. Another objective is to create safe havens in north and east Africa for those genuinely fleeing persecution, rather than migrating for economic reasons.

Both aims offer long-term solutions, but appear immensely difficult to achieve. Nor are they within this government's control.

Even at home, solutions are difficult. Life as an asylum-seeker here can be hard, but compared with the unwelcoming conditions in some European countries Britain remains an appealing destination.

One reason is the English language. Another is the presence here of existing communities from every part of the world. Many have prospered, setting an example today's migrants hope to follow.

Another, less positive, reality is that even those with invalid claims often manage to avoid removal. Some argue that benefits too are a lure.

But as Mrs May knows, in reality most of the solutions are overseas and few are likely to offer rapid relief.

Martin Bentham

30 July 2015

'CALAIS' A GLOBAL CRISIS WITH NO SOLUTION

Everyone is right. Everyone is wrong. Everything has been tried. Nothing works for long. Calais is a never-ending tragedy. After 20 years of "treaties" and "solutions", the cross-Channel migrant crisis is worse than ever.

The number of migrants in Calais - at least 4,000 - has swollen six or seven-fold in the past year. Many of them are veterans of perilous Mediterranean crossings. To reach Libya or Turkey, they endured overland treks through Africa or Asia or the Middle East. They are more hardened, more devil-may-care, more desperate than their patient predecessors.

Hence the aggressive tactics seen in recent weeks. Hence the disturbing surge in the number of migrant deaths this summer - nine in the past month, including a young Sudanese man crushed accidentally by a lorry at the Channel Tunnel freight terminal yesterday morning.

Some of the apocalyptic accounts of this week's events are misleading. There was no mass assault by 2,200 migrants on the Channel Tunnel freight terminal at Coquelles on Monday night. There were repeated breaches of the security fence by groups of 50 migrants at a time.

All the same, migrant attacks on the tunnel freight terminal are at their highest level for many years. The terminal, four miles south of Calais, has been ignored by the migrants in recent times. They preferred to haunt the slip-roads to the ferry port and accost queuing lorries. A security fence, paid for by UK taxpayers, has sealed off these slip-roads in the past couple of weeks. The migrants have been obliged to make the trek to the Chunnel freight terminal instead. New fences are due to be built at Coquelles. The migrants will find a weakness somewhere else.

The Red Cross refugee camp at Sangatte was closed, after British pressure, in 2002. Britain agreed to admit a handful of Bosnians and Kurds. Defence of the UK border was moved, by treaty, across the Channel to Calais (for the first time since the 16th century).

New migrants arrived and lived in squalid camps known as "the jungle" in the dunes and scrubland north of Calais. The jungle was bulldozed in 2009. The migrants now live in new encampments further north ("jungle 2"). After protests by the UN, the French authorities were obliged earlier this year to provide minimal sanitary facilities.

And so it goes on.

The people and politicians of Calais are fed up. The people of Kent are fed up. The lorry drivers are fed up. Some, not all, French politicians say that the British border should be shipped back to Kent. Britain "attracts" the migrants, they say, because it does not have identity cards and because it has a thriving black economy. Let the migrants cross, they say, we have migrant problems of our own.

Some British politicians blame the French. Why don't they just enforce their own laws, arrest all these people and send them home? The French do so, up to a point. The problem is that French courts often refuse repatriations to conflict zones.

Other migrants have Italian-issued papers for the Schengen zone, the border-free area of the continental EU. They have a right to be in France, but have chosen to go to Britain because they speak a little English or have family links in the UK.

The "Calais problem" cannot be solved in Calais because it is not a Calais problem. It is a small part of a European, or world, problem which has no obvious solution either.

When the Calais saga first began some 20 years ago, the migrants were mostly Bosnian refugees from the Yugoslav civil war. They were followed by Iraqis, Pakistanis and Afghans and Somalis - the enterprising flotsam of successive war zones in Europe, Asia and Africa. In many cases, they had invested their life savings with people-smuggling gangs who promised to take them to Britain but dumped them at Calais and pointed vaguely across the Channel. Those migrants observed certain unspoken rules and limits.

Police and volunteer workers say that the latest arrivals in Calais, including many Eritreans, Sudanese and Somalis, are less patient and more determined - and sometimes more aggressive. "There is a change in the mood," one police officer said. "It is partly the sheer numbers but it is also the fact that they have already been through so much before they get here."

Speaking to all the different migrant groups in Calais over the years, it has been impossible not to admire their forbearance and their courage. A steady trickle gets through to the English El Dorado.

The whole depressing circus might be a kind of Jeux sans frontières, or rather Jeux avec frontières, organised by the UK Government to select the most enterprising possible recruits to the British population.

Adamkhan, 34, encountered last year, was a typical case. He was a maths teacher in a primary school in Peshawar, Pakistan. He fled after he and his family were threatened by the Taliban for promoting "Western education".

Speaking in excellent English, he said: "I know the UK is a crowded island and no one wants us. I know the French authorities have a very difficult job. But what is the solution?" If an answer exists, it is not in building bigger fences or bulldozing more camps. Adamkhan and all the others had good reason to leave their homes and risk their lives. The British Government has good reason not to let them all in.

More should be done to prevent these young men from leaving their homes in the first place. And Britain should offer - as it did in 2002 - to take in some of the most deserving and qualified.

Neither is likely to happen. Neither would solve the problem for long if it did happen. That is what makes Calais such a never-ending tragedy. Everyone is right and everyone is wrong.

John Lichfield

August 2015

WHERE IS THE COMPASSION?

Refugees, Keleti Railway Station, Budapest, Hungary, 4 September 2015

3 August 2015

UK URGED TO TAKE IN ASYLUM SEEKERS

Britain was urged to take in more asylum seekers yesterday as fears spread that heightened security in Calais could result in Belgian ports being targeted next.

After Home Secretary Theresa May and her French counterpart Bernard Cazeneuve called on other EU nations to tackle the root causes of the chaos, Sweden's migration minister criticised the UK, suggesting it "could do a lot more" to respond to the crisis.

Morgan Johansson told BBC Radio 4's World This Weekend that the situation in Calais showed "a system that is breaking down" adding the UK doesn't "want to take the responsibility that they should".

Meanwhile, Downing Street announced that the UK will fund additional private security guards, fencing and CCTV cameras to improve security at the terminal in Calais, while more French police are to be deployed to the border over the summer. But that raised fears that the migrants would simply target other European ports such as Zeebrugge in Belgium.

There was also controversy over the cost to taxpayers of housing migrants who have arrived through the tunnel, after contractors Serco confirmed that around 100 were being accommodated in hotels in north-west England as increased numbers outstripped available places in the community.

The Home Office said that the use of hotels was "only ever acceptable as a shortterm contingency measure". Charities also branded the government "morally reprehensible" after the Immigration Minister James Brokenshire launched a new consultation to find ways of removing support from those whose claims have failed, while ensuring mechanisms are in place to protect children.

"The current system should not offer any perverse incentives for illegal migrants to lodge spurious asylum applications," he said.

Migrants can currently obtain accommodation and a £36-a-week support allowance which is removed if their application fails, although those with families continue to receive help.

The Refugee Council's head of advocacy, Lisa Doyle, said the charity had "grave concerns" about the proposals to remove support from "some of the most vulnerable families in the UK".

Another charity, Freedom From Torture, is also opposed to the proposals because "access to adequate welfare meant that families have chance of decent nutrition and well being", a spokeswoman said.

Professor Alexander Betts of the Refugee Studies Centre at the University of Oxford warned they could even risk breaching international human rights laws as people were forced into destitution by the benefits removal.

"There's a basic assumption within human rights law that as a government you have to provide economic rights for people who are on your territory," he said.

"There have been cases in the past of rejected asylum seekers taking governments in Europe to the European Court of Rights and being found against on the basis of destitution," he added.

In essence, Professor Betts said, the proposals could be a violation of international human rights law as it would remove "access to minimum economic rights and leave them in destitution."

Henry Austin

31 August 2015

COMPASSION IS NEEDED

The Great Wall of China, the walls of Rome and every medieval city, the Siegfried Line, the Maginot Line, the Atlantic Wall; nations - empires, dictatorships, democracies - have used every mountain chain and river to keep out foreign armies. And now we Europeans treat the poor and huddled masses, the truly innocent of Syria and Iraq, Afghanistan and Ethiopia, as if they are foreign invaders determined to plunder and subjugate our sovereignty, our heimat, our green and pleasant land.

Barbed wire along the Hungarian border. Barbed wire at Calais. Have we lost the one victory which we Europeans learned from the Second World War - compassion?

Since our latest cliché-rag is to tell the world that the refugee "crisis" is the greatest since that war, I was reminded of how Winston Churchill responded to the German refugee columns fleeing through the snows of eastern Europe in 1945 before the advance of the avenging Soviet Army. These, remember, were the civilians of the Third Reich - those who had brought Hitler to power, who had rejoiced at Nazi Germany's barbaric genocides and military victories over peaceful nations. They were the people of a guilty nation slouching towards Year Zero. It was years since I read the letter Churchill wrote to his wife, Clementine, on his way to the Yalta conference in February of 1945.

But I looked it up this weekend, and here is the key section: "I am free to confess to you that my heart is saddened by the tales of the masses of German women and children flying along the roads everywhere in 40-mile long columns to the West before the advancing armies. I am clearly convinced that they deserve it; but that does not remove it from one's gaze. The misery of the whole world appals me and I fear increasingly that new struggles may arise out of those we are successfully ending." Churchill would have called his sentiment "magnanimity". It was compassion.

Incredibly, it is Germany - the nation from which tens of thousands of refugees fled before the Second World War, and from whose armies they would flee in their millions after the conflict began - which is now the destination of choice for the hundreds of thousands of huddled masses trekking across Europe. Germany's generosity flares like a beacon beside the response of PR Dave and his chums. Didn't our Prime Minister ever read Churchill? Or did he read too much Tennyson? He likes to quote a line from Tennyson's Ulysses - "To strive, to seek, to find, and not to yield" - which was inscribed on the athletes' village wall at the 2012 London Olympic Games. But did he also, I wonder, enjoy Tennyson's own favourite sonnet, Montenegro, in which our Victorian Poet Laureate rejoices at the Montenegrin "warriors beating back the swarm/Of Turkish Islam"? A good word, "swarm". "A good starter but it is a bad sticker," as Churchill himself warned in a pre-war message to Hitler of the Fuhrer's contempt for another benighted people.

More than 30 years ago, in Jerusalem, I met that prince of journalists, James Cameron. He had defended my reporting of Northern Ireland - and so, of course, was a hero of mine - but he, like Churchill, was a man of great compassion. I thought of him not long ago when I was complaining about another group of feral Syrian boy refugees who had been following me down a Beirut street. Almost 40 years ago Cameron was reporting for the BBC on another fleet of refugees seeking salvation on unseaworthy vessels.

"It was a dishonest journalistic compromise to call the Vietnamese refugees the 'boat people'," he wrote in his script, "which has an almost comfortable sound, like people on a holiday cruise. Refugees are fugitives, escapers, victims, the lost and the lonely Jewish refugees, Arab refugees, German refugees, Indian refugees, Pakistani refugees, Russian refugees, Bangladeshi refugees, Korean refugees." Cameron recalled the 17th-century Huguenots who fled to Britain, the persecuted Jews who fled from eastern Europe to America in the 1900s.

And then Cameron came close to a "PR Dave" moment. "In those days the world was a pretty empty place; there was room almost everywhere for the homeless stranger. Everywhere to which an alien might wish to take refuge is now overpopulated, and already with problems of its own." And some refugees "are avaricious, some are saving their skin, some are on a bandwagon. But I have yet to meet a refugee baby who left home other than because he had to". There was no "divine ordinance", Cameron asserted, "that says you must stay where you were born."

Were the followers of Moses not refugees, as they continued to be for 2,000 years, "until they replaced their exodus with someone else's?"

A unique irony of our modern-day tragedy is that an Irish naval vessel has been saving the lives of thousands of shipwrecked refugees a few miles from the Libyan coast. A century and a half ago the Irish famine exodus was washing its refugees up on the coast of Canada, the vessels filled with men, women and children dying or dead of typhus, received with compassion - but also with fear that their plague would contaminate the people of the Canadian Maritimes.

It fell to Pól Ó Muirí, the Irish-language editor of The Irish Times, whose own father was a migrant construction worker in Britain, to point out last week how many Irishmen helped build the Channel Tunnel - and of how today "the migrants are on the other side, trying to get through".

Yes, "something should be done" about the refugees, Ó Muirí rhetorically agreed. But then - and since I love great writing, you must bear with me - he added: "The whole thing is a bit frightening, isn't it, all those people throwing themselves at the fences at the mouth of the tunnel that the Donegal ones helped build. It was when the camera panned back to show men standing and watching, with all the dignity they could muster, that I suddenly realised I was seeing my father in England. Do you see your family in their faces too? Look a little closer. Don't be afraid."

As they say, necessity knows no law. Nor does compassion.

Patrick Cockburn

September 2015

AYLAN AL-KURDI CHANGES ATTITUDES, FOR NOW

Refugees cross Serbian border to Croatia, 18 September 2015

6 September 2015

REFUGEE CRISIS AT A GLANCE

The death by drowning of three-year-old Aylan al-Kurdi last week prompted a conscience-searching moment for Europe. The growing refugee crisis which had been steadily growing on its Mediterranean shores could no longer be ignored.

A young child's death, the latest of thousands who have perished in rickety boats or suffocated in the rear of smugglers' vehicles, may finally have ended the political paralysis on the subject of how to cope with the refugees seeking to escape war and privation in the Middle East and Africa.

Here, The Independent on Sunday provides a graphic illustration of what needs to be done to end the tragedy.

WAVE OR TRICKLE

The European Union's population is roughly 500 million. The latest estimate of the numbers of people using irregular means to enter Europe this year via the Mediterranean or the Balkans is put at approximately 350,000. This amounts to 0.068 percent of the EU's population. Critics claim that given the EU's wealth it hardly lacks the means to absorb these people.

END THE WAR

Experts and politicians agree on one point - peace in Syria and other conflict-stricken countries such as Yemen, Afghanistan and South Sudan - is the surest way to staunch the flood of people seeking safety in Europe.

CUT OUT THE MIDDLE MEN

Officially controlled transfer of migrants from camps surrounding Syria would reduce the risks many of those fleeing to Europe face. Directly controlling the influx also allows European countries to better manage the crisis.

Some countries blame Germany's decision to abandon the EU's Dublin Regulations for the influx. These required people to seek asylum in the first EU state they entered. Germany, which now accepts Syrian asylum-seekers even if they entered the EU elsewhere, said it did so on humanitarian grounds.

Some countries such as Greece and Malta are being overwhelmed by the influx of migrants and refugees. Too few members of the Schengen open borders agreement have been prepared to assist by putting Europe-wide interests above national ones. To survive the Schengen agreement needs to become more flexible in its application.

TERRORISM FEARS

Fears have been raised that terrorists have secreted themselves in the refugee flow. There is no evidence that any have done so. Terror groups have shown themselves adept at recruiting among Europe's own citizens.

BRITAIN

The UK has been castigated both at home and abroad for refusing to accept a European-wide quota solution to the crisis. The government insists its record is better than many. Nearly 5,000 Syrians have been granted asylum in the last four years and the UK has accepted 216 Syrian refugees under a scheme to relocate the most vulnerable begun in early 2014. The Home Office insists 87 percent of initial asylum applications made by Syrians last year were granted. A number of Syrians have also been forcibly removed (145) since 2011 but officials insist none were returned to Syria but instead taken to other "safe" countries through which they had travelled before arriving here.

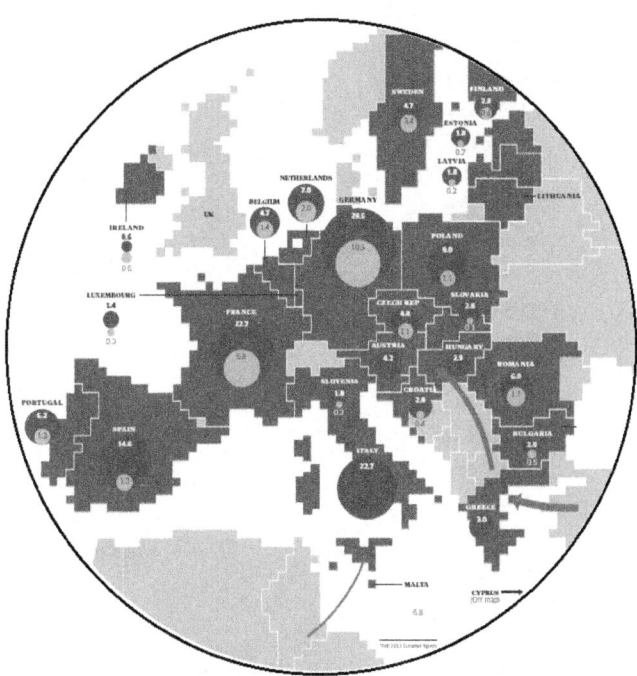

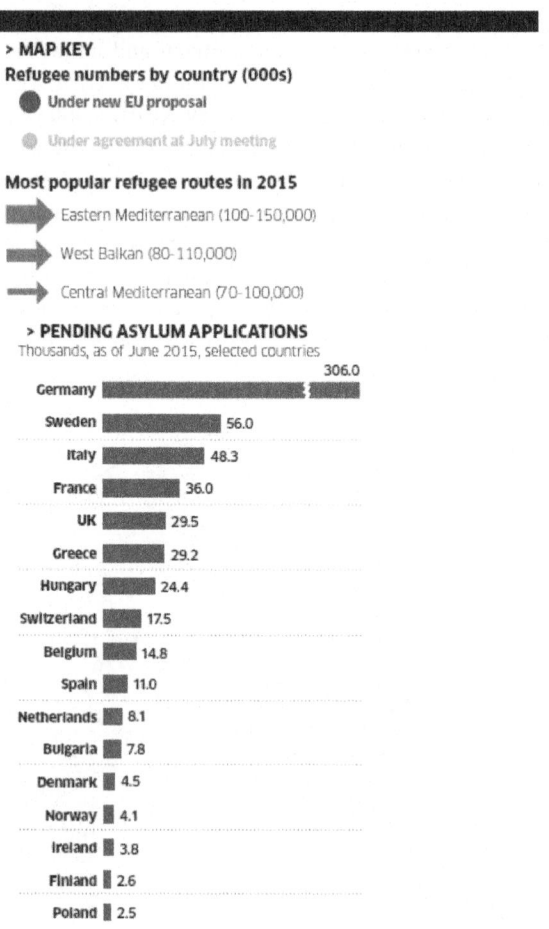

6 September 2015

AYLAN AL-KURDI'S FAMILY RISKS EVERYTHING

The Greek island of Kos had received thousands of refugees and migrants this year, before the images of the body of three-year-old Aylan al-Kurdi sparked shock around the world, again focusing attention on the journeys taken to the island. Alyan's family had taken a boat to reach Kos, but his body, with those of his brother, his mother and numerous others, ended up back on the beach near Bodrum in Turkey Yana (not her real name), 25, from Syria, is mother to two young children, a boy of 11 and a girl of 16 months. For days they have been sleeping in a tent pitched on a roadside in Kos, along with Yana's husband and a cousin. They, too, took a boat from Bodrum, and hope to make it to Germany. Here Yana explains their journey: "We are refugees. We lived in the city of Deir Ezzor. At home there is war - rockets and planes dropping bombs. In Syria, we had no one to defend us against the fighting - no source of protection. In the evenings, we were forbidden to turn the lights on, because otherwise the military planes and helicopters above would bomb us. Then one day the rockets hit the house where we lived. As we escaped, my father was shot in the road.

We left Syria and travelled to Turkey, where we stayed for a month and 10 days. Then we took an overcrowded boat from Bodrum, on the Turkish coast, to Kos. There were about 60 people on this boat, which was meant to hold a maximum of 10 to 15 people. There were eight children and babies on board, all gathered in the middle of the boat, with the adults all around the sides. It was so overcrowded that at one point my baby daughter couldn't breathe.

The crossing took 40 minutes - it was 40 minutes of nightmare. I was so scared, it was as if I saw death. I had to keep my eyes closed. The water was entering the boat and everyone got wet, the children too.

When we arrived on Kos, all our clothes were wet, but we had nothing else to wear, because we had thrown our entire luggage into the sea to make more room on the boat.

I wouldn't make that journey again. Impossible. We took this horrific, dangerous journey because we wanted to make our children's lives easier, safer and better. There is no future in Syria for our children.

We still have family in Syria: my mother, brother and sister are there. They couldn't escape because they don't have the money. It costs a lot of money to get here illegally. We paid the "facilitators" €3,000 (£2,200) for the four of us to make this journey. We hope my mother, brother and sister can escape to be with us.

We were able to contact our family in Syria via [the messaging service] WhatsApp. But it is very dangerous for my family in Syria to access the internet, because Daesh [Islamic State] has stopped all internet access. But there are some secret places where it can be accessed, and my brother managed to go there to learn that we had arrived safely.

Daesh have total control of the city. They take our houses, they take farmers' land, and they say they are now the state. My brother told me that five days ago that Daesh commanded that all women must stay inside their houses and not go out.

As we arrived in Kos with nothing, we have had to buy everything here for ourselves - the tent, which cost €50, clothes for the children, nappies - everything we need. We hope to travel to Germany. [The family will first need to make their way to Athens.] We hope there we will be able to find work and a safe home. Everything we have done has been for our children.

But when the war is over, I want to go back to Damascus - it is beautiful there. We have seen Turkey, we have seen Greece, we are heading to Germany, but I don't want to stay there for ever. I want to return to my Syria. In my mind I have all my memories of life in Syria - it was the best life ever."

Yana spoke to Médecins Sans Frontières (MSF), which is working on the island of Kos.

The Independent

6 September 2015

THE WEEK ATTITUDES CHANGED

MONDAY Hungarian authorities allowed refugees, who had been camped outside Budapest's main train station for weeks, to board trains to Austria and Germany without visa checks.

TUESDAY The station was closed again following chaotic scenes as hundreds packed on to trains for the border. The closure led to street protests outside and thousands started to make their way to Austria on foot.

WEDNESDAY Shocking images of the body of a young boy being recovered from a Turkish beach began to appear on news sites and social media. Turkish media named the boy as three-yearold Syrian, Aylan al-Kurdi, who died with his mother and brother in an ill-fated attempt to reach the Greek island of Kos.

THURSDAY Newspapers put the pictures on their front pages. The Independent printed an image showing Aylan lying facedown in the surf (right).

FRIDAY High-profile figures, including JK Rowling, added their support to calls for refugees to be offered sanctuary.

Bob Geldof described the crisis as a "sickening disgrace" and pledged to accommodate four families.

David Cameron announced Britain will accept "thousands more" Syrian refugees. He said the announcement was a result of the "scale of the crisis and the suffering of the people".

SATURDAY The Refugee Support Network said: "In the past few days we have received more inquiries from members of the public offering to accommodate refugees than in the past five years."

Volunteer organisation CalAid urged people not to drive to Calais, after convoys from Belgium and elsewhere in Europe caused disruption at the French port. They instead asked people to donate through centralised distribution systems.

The Independent

8 September 2015

WILKOMMENSKULUTUR IN MUNICH

Munich's first 20,000 refugees came and went, sent on their way with the good wishes of a city proud to help. Yesterday another 10,000 were expected and the willingness of Munich residents to provide sanctuary appeared to be boundless.

Even as Chancellor Angela Merkel announced yesterday that Germany would set aside some €6bn (£4.3bn) to help fund and accommodate the new arrivals, the residents of one of Europe's richest cities were suddenly face to face with the misery of years of Middle East terror and conflict.

Gisela Hammerl stood on the platform of Munich's Starnberger station with some mobile phone cards. "I was told that that was what the new arrivals needed most," she told The Independent. "Why have I come here? I had to. By comparison I am very wealthy. I want to give all the help I possibly can."

The eagerness to help is so great that the city has been obliged to draw up waiting lists for volunteers who want to assist the flow of refugees and migrants arriving from Hungary and Austria.

Hungary was obliged to let the refugees travel towards Germany last Friday. "There is no end to the exodus in sight," admitted Christoph Hillenbrand, the president of upper Bavaria who is supervising Munich's refugee aid and transport programme. "If it goes on like this we will run out of space," he said. "We are doing everything to make Munich a beacon in Germany," he added. A police spokesman said: "We are expecting around 300 people to arrive every hour."

At the Starnberger station yesterday, some refugees hobbled on worn-out trainers, others brandished placards reading "Thank you Germany". Most smiled with delight, a few struggled to fight back tears.

The first 400 of what promised to be a new wave of refugees began arriving at Munich's main station late yesterday as Europe's biggest refugee crisis since the Second World War entered its second week. As the new arrivals from Syria, Afghanistan and Iraq slowly climbed from an Austrian train, scores of well-wishers burst into applause. Buses took the new arrivals to reception centres to be processed before they are put on trains to new destinations across Germany. At Munich's Riem trade fair complex, 1,700 refugees were put upon camp beds. School and university buildings were also used.

Amid Mohammed, a refugee from Syria with a baby girl in his arms, was one of the many grateful to have made it to Germany. He and his wife took 30 days to flee from Syria via Turkey, Greece and Macedonia. When they arrived in Hungary, they were forced to rough it outside Budapest's Keleti railway station for seven days. "It was terrible," said Mr Mohammed. "I love Germany." Speaking after meeting with heads of Germany's federal states, Angela Merkel described the past week as "breathtaking", adding that it had "provided an image of Germany we can be proud of". But in a remark directed at Germany's EU partners, she added: "The time for a joint solution is upon us."

Despite the euphoria that has accompanied Germany's new-found Wilkommenskulutur, or "Welcome culture", far-right activists have continued their violent opposition. There have been more than 200 attacks on refugee hostels in Germany this year. On Sunday night neo-Nazis were suspected of setting fire to containers housing 84 asylum-seekers in Rottenburg, in south-west Germany. Five people were injured.

Germany's federal states have agreed new measures to help deal with the crisis. They include strengthening police forces with 3,000 new recruits and speeding up deportation for economic migrants from Montenegro, Albania and Kosovo, which are considered safe countries. Almost half of all migrants to Germany this year have been Kosovo Albanians. Germany is giving priority to war refugees from Syria, Afghanistan and Iraq.

Despite widespread public support for Ms Merkel's welcome policy for refugees, she continued to face angry protests from her Bavarian conservative coalition partners yesterday. Horst Seehofer, head of Bavaria's Christian Social Union, said Chancellor Merkel has sent "completely the wrong signal" by welcoming refugees. "No society can accept this sort of influx in the long term," he insisted.

Jean-Claude Juncker, President of the European Commission, has drawn up plans for a fair distribution of refugees across the EU which envisages Germany, France and Spain bearing the brunt of the intake. Under his proposals, Germany will take in a further 31,500 migrants and refugees followed by France with 24,000 and Spain with 15,000.

Tony Paterson

14 September 2015

REFUGEES CONTRIBUTE TO ECONOMIES

It's clear where Roy "Chubby" Brown stands on the subject of refugee economics. "I am asylum seeker, we love all your benefits/You give us a house, car, money, NHS, and a glimpse of Jordan's tits" the obscene comedian bellows in one of his charming ditties.

Chubby Brown doesn't, mercifully, speak for Britain. Nevertheless this impression of refugees as an economic drain on the host community - as people who take but don't give - is a depressingly common one.

It helps to explain why opinion polls still show a majority are against the UK accepting more refugees from Syria, despite pleas from the United Nations for European nations to do more, and even in the face of tragedies such as the drowning of threeyear-old Aylan Kurdi in the Mediterranean as his family tried to reach Europe.

The idea that refugees are an economic burden is a myth. The evidence we have suggests the opposite. Of course, in the immediate term it does cost taxpayers money to shelter and feed the traumatised people who manage to escape violence and persecution in their home countries. But in the medium and long-term the evidence we have suggests that people fleeing across national borders for their safety generally end up contributing disproportionately to economic growth and living standards.

Research from Uganda, which has a large population of refugees from countries such as Congo and South Sudan, shows that asylum-seekers there are intimately plugged into the local economy as traders, consumers and business owners. In Kenya, proposals to shut down the giant Kakuma refugee camp, which hosts displaced people from 15 neighbouring countries, in the early 2000s provoked uproar from the local host community, similar to the outcry we see in the UK when a local hospital is threatened with the axe. Kenyans saw the camp as a major source of employment and commercial opportunities.

These are pertinent examples because there are far more refugees in developing countries than in rich ones. Amid the hysterical coverage of the refugee crisis in Europe it is often overlooked that of Syria's four million refugees, two million are in Turkey and one million are in Lebanon.

But what about rich countries? Evidence from Australia (where attitudes towards refugees often make Chubby Brown sound like a spokesman for Amnesty International) suggests that refugees are more likely than other migrants to be entrepreneurs. A disproportionate number of asylumseekers Down Under within a few years end up relying on income from their own unincorporated businesses.

There are many other examples of political refugees making a heroic economic contribution to their new homes. The influx of mainland Chinese into Hong Kong, fleeing first the Japanese invasion in the 1940s and then the economic lunacy of Mao in the 1950s, helped to power the British colony's phenomenal success in the postwar years.

Among the refugees was a young boy called Li Ka-Shing. He built a great business empire and is one of Asia's richest men.

Here in the UK an outstanding example of entrepreneurial refugees are the 40,000 Ugandan Asians who were admitted in the 1970s after the mass expulsion by Idi Amin.

Going back further, the tale of Michael Marks is one that deserves to be highlighted. He was a Jewish child from Belarus, then part of the Russian empire. He came to Leeds to escape the Tsarist pogroms in 1882. He worked for a tailoring factory in the city that employed Jewish asylum-seekers. Later he opened a penny bizarre market stall, and after that went into business with Thomas Spencer. If Britain hadn't admitted this Jewish refugee we would today have no Marks & Spencer.

It's not surprising that refugees often make a large economic contribution. Not everyone flees, even in the face of repression or death. As well as desperation, it often requires a certain level of determination and courage. Those that make it are often natural risk-takers.

Furthermore, the dictators and sectarian thugs that drive out communities tend not to be economically clued up about the human capital they are depriving themselves of. The imbecilic Amin is said to have expelled Uganda's Asians after a bad dream.

This means that quite often refugees are educated, bringing with them skills that can be put to use in their new homes. Hitler drove out scores of brilliant Jewish scientists from Germany in the 1930s. Sir Ian Jacob, one of Winston Churchill's aides, is said to have joked that the Allies won the Second World War because "our German scientists were better than their German scientists".

The idea that there is a major refugee "pull factor" from the rich world's welfare states is unsubstantiated. If anything, the pull factor seems to be the work opportunities on offer. Why are asylumseekers who have arrived in Hungary so desperate to depart for Germany? Because they have a desire, ultimately, to work for a living, and Germany, rather than Hungary, provides that opportunity.

In truth, the distinction between economic migrants and refugees is not so clear cut. Many want to seek sanctuary in rich countries precisely because they do not want to be helpless refugees forever.

It's worth noting that, even in the immediate term, if immigrants arrive in sufficient numbers their presence can be economically helpful. The distribution of humanitarian aid boosts government spending. Germany's budget surplus this year will be smaller because of its government's decision to welcome 800,000 asylum-seekers.

That will help growth and result in a loosening of Berlin's excessively tight fiscal policy. Thus we have a rare example of Angela Merkel's government doing something macroeconomically sensible. The newcomers - equal to 1 per cent of Germany's population - will also help to ease the country's long-term demographic crisis.

As for Britain, when it comes to refugees, our own government often seems to do the wrong thing for the wrong reasons. A salient example is the tight restrictions on asylum seekers finding work. It must seem a Kafkaesque nightmare to refugees to be criticised for relying on benefits while being obstructed by the law from providing for themselves.

The debate about the admittance of refugees should not, of course, be dominated by economic concerns. Morality, justice and culture are, quite rightly, the dominant part of the mix. But the argument that we should refuse to accept our share of the world's refugees because we can't afford it is as feeble as Chubby Brown's brand of humour.

Ben Chu

15 September 2015

REFUGEES RUSH TO ENTER HUNGARY AS DOOR SHUTS

Almost 26 years since the day, in 1989, when Hungary opened its borders to citizens of East Germany, heralding the collapse of the Iron Curtain, those same barriers are being closed. In a desperate effort to stem the flow of asylum seekers fleeing war zones in Syria, Iraq, Afghanistan and beyond, the Hungarian government yesterday deployed flanks of police and soldiers wielding automatic weapons to patrol its border with Serbia, assisted by a 110-mile long newly constructed barbed-wire fence. According to new legislation effective from today, entering Hungary illegally will constitute a criminal act, potentially punishable by a prison sentence of up to three years. Yesterday afternoon police closed the unofficial crossing along a train track between the Serbian village of Horgos and Roszke in Hungary, a route previously popular with refugees.

The news seemed to have spread to refugees, many from Syria, who quickened their pace to reach Hungary, with police recording 6,000 entering on Sunday and a further 5,353 arrivals even before

11am on Monday. Many were transported by train from Roszke to Hegyeshalom on the Austrian border. The United Nations refugee agency claimed that not all were being registered, claims denied by the Hungarian government. "Where are we going now?" asked Abdullah Faraj, a Syrian physician as he queued up to board a bus. Mr Faraj, 28, from Deir Ezzor, the city currently caught in the middle of raging battles between government forces and Isis militants, spoke as a helicopter flew overhead. He and his four friends had heard about the Hungarian border closing and had raced across the Balkans to reach Roszke after leaving Syria only a week ago. "I read on the news about the border being blocked, so we didn't sleep on our journey, maybe a few hours. I want to get to Austria and start working. In Deir Ezzor I was treating patients in critical situations, burns, victims of bombing but each day it gets worse, and there is no safety. I want to keep helping people in Austria." Mr Faraj still has friends currently en route to western Europe and wonders how their path will change now. He said: "We heard that other countries like Croatia or Slovenia might open up for refugees."

On the train tracks the silence was punctuated by workers stapling brackets into the fence and a swarm of media filmed horses trotting past carrying police and refugees on the Serbian side.

Husam Haffi, 44, a Palestinian-Syrian bank worker from the Yarmouk refugee camp in Syria, was one of the last to cross. He smoked his first cigarette in three days, surrounded by his four children and wife. Days ago they braved the perilous sea crossing from Turkey to Greece that on Sunday claimed the lives of 34 refugees. "Back home we were living on the fourth floor, and now that is on the ground. Nothing."

Mr Haffi and his family previously tried living in Ain el-Hilweh, the largest Palestinian refugee camp in Lebanon, but found conditions intolerable. "Everybody has guns, people kill each other for a piece of chocolate. It's not life."

In the last week the cornfield by the tracks in Roszke has become an international focal point of the crisis as sporadic transportation to overcapacity registration centres saw swelling numbers of asylum seekers effectively kettled under open skies. There have been daily tensions between refugees and police as many became angered at the long waiting times and lack of adequate shelter. Yesterday, large tents provided by the UNHCR and other organisations that were finally erected, stood empty as the trickle of refugees ceased.

UNCHR spokesman Babar Baloch wandered along the road by the fence where families of refugees could be seen through the barbed wire on the other side. He told The Independent: "Whenever there is an obstacle to a refugee population, it endangers their lives and compels them to take dangerous routes with traffickers and we have seen what happens when they give themselves up to the traffickers. Europe cannot turn back people who are fleeing wars and conflicts."

At the bus queue, Mr Haffi points to his two-year-old daughter Nirvana. "They can take me back across the border if they want, I just want good health and education for her. My kids didn't have school in two years. They are happy now because we are together, but I will tell them all about this when they are older."

Andrew Connelly

17 September 2015
HUNGARY SLAMS DOOR – CROATIA OFFERS NEW ROUTE

Hundreds of people crossed into Croatia last night as the country countered Hungary's decision to close its borders to those refugees making their way across Europe - providing an alternative route towards Germany and Austria.

Having mostly failed to penetrate Hungary's newly erected border fortifications with Serbia - even before the clashes that erupted yesterday - refugees were bused to the Serbian town of Sid, a few miles from the Croatian border, and began crossing into the European Union on foot.

The majority of the refugees were believed to be women and children and there were reports that some were taken by taxis to the border. "They will be able to pass through Serbia and we will help them to do so," insisted Croatia's Prime Minister Zoran Milanovic. "We are ready to lead the people towards where they apparently want to go - Germany or Scandinavia," he added.

To the north, Vesna Gyorkos Znidar, the Interior Minister of neighbouring Slovenia - another step on the way to Germany - said yesterday that the country would not simply let migrants and refugees pass through, but would receive claims for asylum. Croatia joined the EU in 2013 but the country has not signed up to the EU's Schengen agreement on open borders.

Many of the refugees had chosen to cross into Croatia on foot and across open maize fields in the border region. Reports in Croatia yesterday said the Serbian and Macedonian authorities were jointly arranging alternative transport for refugees who had been trying to enter the EU via Hungary. Both countries were said to have agreed that refugees and migrants travelling on the west Balkan route from Turkey should be bused directly from Macedonia to Serbia's border with Croatia.

Having already constructed a fence across its border with Serbia, yesterday Hungary's Prime Minister Viktor Orban intimated that the country will build a fence along parts of its border with Croatia, and also Romania. "We have decided to build a fence also on the border with Romania," Mr Orban told Austrian newspaper Die Presse. "We will also erect a fence at certain locations on the Croatian border," he said.

In an effort to slow the number of refugees coming into Europe, which has reached 500,000 this year, Germany and Austria began enforcing controls on their southern borders at the weekend, and yesterday Germany closed a rail link that has brought tens of thousands of people in from Austria in less than two weeks. This caused chaotic scenes at Austria's Salzburg train station where travel between there and Germany was halted in both directions. Many refugees were prevented from continuing on their desired journey, leading to an exodus from the station and several hundred walking towards the German border a few miles away.

Austria also extended its own toughened border checks - introduced on the border with Hungary yesterday morning - to its frontier with Slovenia to the south, expecting refugees and migrants to find their way around the blockades in Hungary.

In Berlin, Chancellor Angela Merkel insisted that Germany would continue to open its doors to refugees despite criticism from rightwingers in her party who have argued that her policies have only exacerbated the crisis. In an emotional response to her critics, Ms Merkel said yesterday: "I have to say quite honestly that if now I have to start apologising for showing a friendly face in an emergency, then this is not my country."

Despite Monday's failure of EU interior ministers to agree on a quota system to share out some 160,000 refugees across the continent, Ms Merkel appears to be still banking on achieving a Europe-wide solution to the problem at an emergency meeting of EU leaders next week.

Thomas de Maizière, her Interior Minister, has suggested that the east European EU member states which have strongly opposed quotas should be punished by being subjected to cuts in the structural funding they receive from Brussels.

Mr Orban said that if the EU decides to impose mandatory quotas of asylum-seekers on member states, his country would have to comply. "Then it would be law and we'd have to accept it," he said, although he added he was only prepared to talk about the quota system if it was on a voluntary basis.

Germany has set aside €6bn for the crisis. However, the leaders of all of the country's 16 federal states and most town and regional council heads have complained that they do not have the resources to meet the scale of the problem.

As a first step, Germany has agreed to set up special transit centres to manage the distribution of refugees. Ms Merkel wants Greece and Italy to set up so-called "hot spots" which are capable of distinguishing between genuine war refugees and economic migrants. Along with other EU leaders, Ms Merkel also wants to improve conditions for Syrian refugees in Turkey and Jordan.

MINEFIELDS LEGACY OF BALKAN CONFLICT

As people made their way from Serbia to Croatia yesterday, they faced the added danger of possible unexploded landmines.

The border between the two nations saw fighting during the 1991 to 1995 war as Croatia split from federal Yugoslavia, with thousands of landmines part of the legacy of that conflict.

Yesterday the Croatian government said demining experts working in the east of the country had been sent with police to ensure that all minefields had been properly marked.

Croatia's Mine Action Centre says there are around 190 square miles of hazardous areas - containing around 50,000 landmines. Hundreds of people have been killed or injured by mines since the conflict ended. Miljenko Vahtaric, an official at the centre, said that there are five suspected mine areas near the border with Serbia.

Aid groups in Croatia and Hungary were working yesterday to try and make those crossing into Croatia aware of the potential dangers, as well as advising people to stick to main roads and avoid walking through woodland. Médecins Sans Frontières, one of those aid groups, called for "safe and legal routes" for refugees so they do not stray into minefields. Groups such as Migration Aid Hungary, a collection of volunteers, posted maps of areas where landmines might be present.

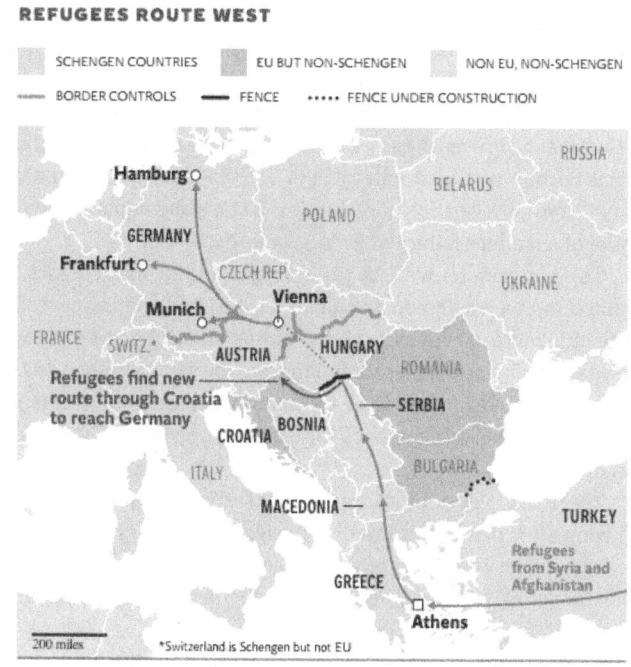

REFUGEES ROUTE WEST

Tony Paterson

19 September 2015

EUROPE'S DARK NATIONALISM IS BACK

Refugees packed into trains and told they are being taken abroad to safety but ending up in a camp. Migrants refused entry on the grounds of religion. Uncomprehending victims of persecution having identity numbers inked onto their arms. Walls being assembled across the continent. And an abject failure of supposedly civilised, cultured and rich nation states to work together.

Yes, as has been much observed in recent weeks, there are many echoes across Europe of darker, uglier episodes from the past. One would not want to make too much of them - it would be highly disrespectful to victims of the Holocaust - but there have been some nasty reminders that liberal democratic values are not as well entrenched in Europe as we might wish.

It will be 70 years ago next year that Winston Churchill, recently unseated as prime minister and at a loose end, travelled to Fulton, Missouri, and uttered his famous warning that: "From Stettin in the Baltic to Trieste in the Adriatic, an iron curtain has descended across the Continent." It was already too late; the Soviet occupation of east-central Europe was well entrenched. Today's curtain of razor wire doesn't have such neat termini, but it is a stark and equally powerful symbol of a modern failure of European unity.

The barriers, as well as the tear gas and armoured cars and squalid camps, are a demonstration of the durability and appeal of the nineteenth-century construct of the "nation state". No appeals to European solidarity or the rights of man have the same potency as a call to defend national borders. Even Germany has decided to re-establish its border with Austria. So much for Schengen. So much for the European dream.

There are plenty more signs that the nation state is alive and well, long after it was supposedly consigned to history. A flag, a culture, a language and sense of allegiance remain powerful adhesives, either for an existing, strong nation state, or one that is still being formed or reformed.

Years ago the leaders of Germany, France, Italy, the Netherlands, Belgium and Luxembourg held a conference at Messina in Sicily that laid the foundations for the European Community, now the European Union. The ideals have been well canvassed: that nations that trade together stay at peace together. It has, indeed, delivered peace in Western Europe for all that time - no mean feat - and added immeasurably to the prosperity and happiness of the continent.

It has even succeeded in its rather dated idea of allowing Europe to be strong in a world of giant blocs. It has grown to the present community of 28 member states and 500 million citizens. It has a flag, and a nice joyful anthem by Beethoven. And yet, as we have seen in recent weeks, when the chips are down, European ideals count for nothing. If Hungary wants to stick a fence up, it will.

And while the welcoming arms of Germany and Austria have been opened wide for Syrian refugees, those same states negotiated special opt-out clauses to prevent Poles, Bulgarians and Romanians from coming over to get jobs. Not to mention multiple breaches of EU Directives by the French. The European project has not extinguished chauvinism in Europe; heavens, even Belgium, the centre of its institutions, can barely hold together as a single nation state, its Flemish and Walloon elements pulled apart by the magnetic force of two established nation states either side: France and Holland.

The EU is not, of course, the USSR or Yugoslavia. Many of the fragments of those conglomerates still want to join the EU: Serbia, Ukraine, Macedonia. They, superficially at least, want to pool sovereignty. But we have witnessed that when something visceral happens, their nationalism is on a hair trigger. It is difficult to see them sharing a government with France, Ireland and Finland. Europe lacks a common media, a common political discourse, a common language - all of which would be more use than a single currency.

Europe isn't even a "tribe with a flag", as an Egyptian diplomat dismissed some of his Arab neighbours. The EU will never be a nation state. Will Britain remain one? It's obviously not such an odd question any longer. Over not much more than a decade, England has not-so-quietly re-emerged as a "nation", after many centuries of dormancy (outside of sport, which is perhaps the best indicator of the ability of a nation to stick together). When there was all that fuss Jeremy Corbyn not singing the national anthem last week, it was really a debate about nationhood.

Sean O'Grady

October 2015

GERMANY STRAINED

"Refugees Welcome", Berlin, Germany, 16 September 2015

8 October 2015

GERMANY'S 'WELCOME CULTURE' FADES

Inside a converted Oktoberfest beer tent at the back of Passau's train station 300 bewildered and exhausted refugees sat penned behind steel barriers as they awaited so-called "Fast ID" registration.

They were the latest to arrive in the German town on Austria's border which has become one of the main entry points for migrants. As two young voluntary workers tried to hand out drinks, a group of Syrians and their small children suddenly stood up and started to move towards the beer tent door and a waiting bus outside.

But this act of apparent insubordination was too much for one uniformed police officer, who leapt on to a bench and screamed: "Sit down! Don't move!"Worn out by weeks of refugee duty, his temper had snapped. The refugee children started crying. Passau's railway station has a sign proclaiming: "Refugees Welcome". But apart from the police, there was no one to greet the thousands of migrants arriving this week. "It's not like a month ago when lots of ordinary people would come and applaud when they arrived," admitted Commissioner Albert Poerschke, the city's police spokesman on refugees. "The welcome culture seems to have evaporated. We waiting for the rest of Europe to help us solve the crisis," he told The Independent.

The absence of this "welcome culture", which Chancellor Angela Merkel called for at the start of the refugee crisis in September was also palpable on the streets of Passau - an idyllic 18th-century Danube town dubbed "Bavaria's Venice". Anton, a hotel receptionist, who did not want to reveal his surname was adamant: "Of course we have to help them, but I think we will lose our German culture if they don't stop coming in. It is too much. Maybe we would build a wall around Passau," he told The Independent.

Since Germany started introducing police controls on its borders with Austria and the Czech Republic in mid-September, the Bavarian border towns of Passau and Rosenheim have borne the brunt of Germany's refugee influx. According to a leaked government report, the number of asylum applications is expected to reach 1.5 million this year - almost double the estimated 800,000.

Bavaria alone has taken in 225,000 refugees since the beginning of September. Almost half have passed through Passau, which is accepting between 1,000 and 5,000 new arrivals each day. Jürgen Dupper, the city's Social Democrat mayor describes the town's predicament as "very, very dramatic" and has demanded better border controls. Yet the influx shows no sign of abating.

A survey of Syrian refugees who have made it to Germany concluded yesterday that the main reason for their flight was fear of President Bashar al-Assad. More than 90 per cent were fleeing the fighting, with two-thirds blaming the Assad government. Only 32 per cent said they were fleeing Isis.

One-third of the refugees arrive in Germany by train; the rest enter from Austria by road, and often on foot. The Austrians are reported to be handing each refugee a map showing where the German border is. "Many ask us whether they are in Australia," an Austrian police spokesman was quoted as saying. "About 80 percent of the Syrian and Afghan refugees don't know where or what Austria is. That's why they want to go to Germany," he added.

But opinion polls suggest the German public is becoming increasingly frustrated at what many see as the failure of Ms Merkel's government to stem the influx. A survey published on Monday by Germany's Market and Social Research group showed that 59 per cent of Germans thought Ms Merkel was wrong to allow refugees to arrive unhindered from Hungary at the end of August. A month ago 66 percent thought the Chancellor was doing the right thing. The polls also show that a large majority of Germans now want the influx stopped.

Ms Merkel is also under intense political pressure to end her "open door" refugee policy. This week an open letter signed by 34 of her conservative MPs and state politicians complained that the refugee crisis was becoming unbearable. On Tuesday, Ms Merkel announced plans to set up a special refugee crisis unit.

Whether the measure will better the lot of Syrian refugees like 30-year-old Ali Nabo is questionable. After a three week journey with his wife and three young daughters from the Syrian city of Homs, he stood in a filthy coat in the Oktoberfest beer tent. He and his family had to ditch all their belongings during their sea crossing from Turkey to Greece as they feared their rubber boat would sink. Now he was worried he would be separated from his wife and children. What seemed like the first big smile for a long time shone from his face when a policeman reassured him: "We don't split up families."

Tony Paterson

12 October 2015

TIDE TURNING AGAINST MERKEL

When a disgruntled member of Angela Merkel's ruling Christian Democrats attempted a weak jibe at the German leader's open-door refugee policy, he asked her why she had not already set up tents for migrants in front of the Reichstag in Berlin.

Ms Merkel's response was disarmingly honest. She said a refugee camp in front of the Reichstag might upset the tourists who visit the building each day. "Anyway, they would think Merkel had gone crazy," she added.

Clearly hoping that the rest of the European Union would come to her aid, in this respect Ms Merkel finds herself disappointed, left in the lurch and almost alone. In recent days it has appeared as if the refugee crisis she is accused of helping ignite with a "selfie" of herself with a migrant in September, has run out of control.

Ms Merkel has dismissed charges that it encouraged thousands of predominantly Syrian and Afghan refugees to head for Germany in particular, although reports from Berlin's embassies on the west Balkan route are said to have suggested otherwise.

"Do you think that hundreds of thousands of people would leave their homes and embark on this difficult road just because of a selfie with the Chancellor?" Ms Merkel said at the weekend. She does not like the idea that it helped spark Europe's refugee crisis. But her political future now rests almost entirely on whether she can meet the challenge - the biggest her country has faced since the fall of the Berlin Wall.

Apart from those on the farright there are few in Germany at the moment who would be prepared to say that Ms Merkel has taken leave of her senses. Yet with the country facing a potential influx of some 1.5 million migrants this year alone, the number of those who think that she has gone too far and too fast with her refugee policies is rapidly rising. The "welcome culture" that saw thousands of Germans greet refugees from Syria and Afghanistan in September has all but evaporated. A poll published yesterday by the Emnid Institute showed that 49 per cent of Germans now think Ms Merkel's refugee policy is wrong; 39 per cent approve. At the start of the crisis, the figures were the other way around.

The public's growing disapproval is mirrored by political unease. Hardly a day goes by without Ms Merkel being attacked by the head of a party who should be her close political ally. Horst Seehofer, the Bavarian prime minister and leader of the state's conservative Christian Social Union, has banned Ms Merkel from his party's annual conference because of fear that she might be "booed down".

Bavaria has so far borne the brunt of the crisis. An estimated 175,000 refugees entered Germany via the southern German state last month. Mr Seehofer has complained that "no society can cope with an influx on this scale". He is now threatening to take Ms Merkel to Germany's Constitutional Court.

The Chancellor's Social Democrat coalition partners agree: "We cannot go on continually taking in more than a million refugees each year and trying to integrate them," complained the Social Democrat leader Sigmar Gabriel and Ms Merkel's Social Democrat Foreign Minister Frank-Walter Steinmeier. Even the respected President, the former East German dissident Joachim Gauck, has not minced his words: "Our capacity to take in refugees is limited, even if the limits have not yet been negotiated," he said in a speech.

The number of far-right attacks on refugee camps is growing. Thousands are attending protest rallies organised by anti-immigration groups such as the Alternative for Germany party. In Austria yesterday, the farright Freedom Party made huge gains in city elections in Vienna after an anti-refugee campaign, according to initial exit poll results. However, it appeared to have narrowly failed to oust the ruling Social Democrats.

Where does all this leave Ms Merkel? The Chancellor went on prime-time German television last week and told viewers that there could be no halt to the influx without effectively building another Berlin Wall. "Building fences around Germany will not help," she insisted. At the same time she stuck to her mantra: "Wir schaffen das" (We will manage this).

Margaret Heckel, one of Ms Merkel's several biographers, says she is convinced that she took the decision to let in the refugees on the spur of the moment and probably alone. "Since reunification Germany has been under mounting pressure from her allies to take on more global responsibility, this was a chance for Angela Merkel to show that Germany could do something," she told The Independent.

The Chancellor herself has admitted that a Germany that turned away refugees "would not be the Germany I want".

Ms Merkel's principled and altruistic motives may well have been determined by her upbringing as the daughter of a Protestant pastor in communist East Germany who devoted much of his life to helping the mentally ill. At the same time she is acting on the fact that Germany's rapidly ageing population means that the country is in need of young immigrants.

In an effort to show that she was firmly back in the driving seat last week, she set up a special refugee crisis unit which is being run from her own Chancellery. Yesterday the minister in charge of the unit said Germany would aim to set up transit camps at the country's borders to send back unwanted migrants.

Tony Paterson

14 October 2015

BORDER 'TRANSIT ZONES'

Chancellor Angela Merkel's plans for controversial border "transit zones" to slow the pace of refugees entering Germany has divided her ruling coalition - and opposition MPs have likened them to frontier "concentration camps" for unwanted migrants.

Ms Merkel's Interior Minister, Thomas de Maiziere, and the head of her new migrant crisis unit, Peter Altmaier, proposed at the weekend zones from which Germany could speedily repatriate unwanted economic migrants to "safe" countries.

The transit zones are seen as an attempt to convince an increasingly nervous German public that after weeks of apparent indecision, Ms Merkel's government has come up with workable proposals to slow down a refugee influx predicted to exceed one million by the end of this year. Some 40 per cent of those entering Germany prove to be economic refugees, from countries such as Albania.

Bavaria, which has borne the brunt of refugee arrivals, has been at the forefront of demands for transit zones.

The proposal came against a backdrop of rising anger on the right, with a rebirth of Germany's xenophobic Pegida (Patriotic Europeans Against Islamisation of the West) movement. On Monday 9,000 supporters held an anti-refugee rally in the movement's home city of Dresden. Protesters brandished makeshift "gallows" with "nooses reserved" for Ms Merkel and her deputy, Sigmar Gabriel.

Yesterday, the EU's border agency reported that 170,000 migrants had been detected entering in September, down slightly from the record 190,000 in August but bringing this year's total recorded influx to 710,000 so far.

But the likelihood of the German zones ever being realised dimmed significantly yesterday. Heiko Maas, Germany's Social Democrat Justice Minister, said he opposed the idea. Warning of legal complications, he said the proposal would create "mass camps in no-man's land". Yasmin Fahimi, his party's general secretary, said the plan was "unworkable." The opposition Free Democrat politician Wolfgang Kubicki said the transit zones would amount to de facto "concentration camps".

The idea was also denounced by Wolfgang Neskovic, a former high court judge. He told Berlin's Inforadio news station that the plan was incompatible with the Schengen agreement on free movement, which envisaged that such transit zones would be confined to the EU's external frontiers. "Politically the idea is a failure at birth," he said.

Horst Seehofer, Bavaria's right-wing conservative leader, said he still backed the idea. Ms Merkel has herself been obliged to admit that the transit zones would only work in certain cases.

She has declined to set an upper limit for the number of refugees her government is prepared to accept, maintaining Germany can cope with the influx. She says the issue needs to be addressed by the rest of Europe and in the Middle East. On Sunday she will visit Turkey to seek Ankara's assistance in overcoming the crisis.

Tony Paterson

17 October 2015

FIRST REFUGEE TO BE SHOT DEAD

An as-yet-unnamed 25-yearold man has become the first refugee to be shot dead trying to enter the European Union when he was struck by a bullet fired by a Bulgarian border guard. The young Afghan, who died on Thursday night, had been among 54 refugees making their way to a better life in Europe when two guards tried to stop them.

He may be just one of thousands to perish on the hazardous journey westwards this year, and just one soul among the more than 700,000 refugees to seek asylum in the EU. But his death is a shocking illustration of the irony that, even as the EU opens its gates to refugees, it is adding guards to these gates.

The young Afghan's death is just one element in the whirling vortex of Europe's refugee crisis, but it is a particularly grim landmark. Officials say he was probably killed by a stray bullet that ricocheted off the bridge under which he was hiding, near the town of Sredets in south-east Bulgaria - around 20 miles from the border with

Turkey, a country that has become pivotal to the EU's response to the crisis.

Within Bulgaria, the death prompted widely different reactions. Atanas Atanassov, the chair of the parliamentary committee on internal security and a minority partner in the coalition government, said: "In such a situation, we are talking about murder." But Valeri Simeonov, co-leader of the nationalist Patriotic Front, took a contrasting stance. "The Bulgarian border police officers should be given medals because they were doing their job," he said.

Such opposing opinions are reflected across the EU, where the refugee crisis has stirred both generous humanity and ugly insularity. At the moment the Afghan was shot, EU leaders were meeting on the opposite edge of the continent in Brussels to discuss their refugee policy. Upon hearing the news, the Bulgarian Prime Minister Boyko Borisov left the summit and headed home.

It meant that Mr Borisov missed the grand declarations at the summit's conclusion about new measures to deal with the crisis. The Prime Minister David Cameron and other leaders agreed to ease visa restrictions for Turkey's 78 million citizens and speed up EU entry talks as part of a deal aimed at securing Turkey's support in stemming the flood of refugees westwards.

With 2.5 million Syrians currently in refugee camps on Turkish soil, Ankara's cooperation is essential in preventing an exodus into the EU. The European Council President Donald Tusk, chairing the fourth Brussels summit on the refugee crisis in six months, said an agreement with Turkey "makes sense only if it contains the flow of refugees".

The broader refugee plan involves beefing up border controls, returning unwanted migrants, and giving the EU's border agency Frontex more power to expel rejected asylum-seekers. Patrolling the EU's external borders will be crucial. Bulgaria has built a 20-mile razor-wire fence along part of its porous 160-mile frontier with Turkey, and sent some 2,000 border guards, police and troops to guard the rest. Hungary, meanwhile, said yesterday it had finished building a barrier along its border with Croatia, a much used migrant crossing point, and would seal the border to migrants at midnight.

But Turkey is the key to any successful refugee plan. While the leaders did not agree on any firm aid figure, the German Chancellor Angela Merkel, who has faced a public opinion backlash for her pro-refugee stance, said afterwards that the EU was considering a €3bn (£2.2bn) package - which would still be less than half the €7bn that Turkey has spent hosting Syrian refugees. "In the future we have to be stronger on burden sharing," she said.

Even so, the Turkish President Recep Tayyip Erdogan mocked the EU's contribution yesterday. "They announce they'll take in 30,000 to 40,000 refugees and then they are nominated for the Nobel for that. We're hosting two and a half million refugees but nobody cares," Mr Erdogan said, referring to the EU's 2012 Nobel Peace Prize win.

Any agreement would depend on Ankara dismantling the criminal networks that smuggle migrants, and agreeing to take back migrants who transit Turkey but are denied EU refugee status.

The negotiations come as Turkey is gearing up for parliamentary elections on 1 November. The EU has criticised Mr Erdogan's increasing authoritarianism and its leaders are wary of granting him a preelection propaganda coup. Yet they feel they have little choice but to play his game: with more dead children washing up on Greek beaches, the prospect of still more Syrian refugees has concentrated their minds. A European Commission progress report, expected to be critical of developments in Turkey and due to be released this week, has been postponed until after the elections.

Leo Cendrowicz

November 2015

TERRORISTS FEARED TO BE AMONG THEM

Syrian migrants arrive from Turkey to Lesbos, Greece, 29 October 2015

6 November 2015

GREECE UNABLE TO COPE

Confronted by the thousands of migrants and refugees stranded on the island of Lesbos, the Greek Prime Minister, Alexis Tsipras, was forced to concede yesterday that his country was unable to cope with the unprecedented influx.

"I think we are battling something which is beyond our abilities, and everyone should understand that," he said on a visit to a packed migrant registration centre with Martin Schulz, head of the European Parliament.

As overloaded dinghies continue to be sent across the Aegean by Turkish smugglers - a journey that cost three children their lives this week - Mr Tsipras was met at the gates of the Moria camp by around 100 protesters, who were wearing life jackets and brandishing placards calling on the European Union to stop deaths by allowing refugees safe and legal passage to Europe.

Two students were among the demonstrators after deciding to use the start of their gap year to volunteer on Lesbos. Annie Risner, 18, said she had seen the camp being cleaned and the shrubbery being trimmed ahead of the Greek Prime Minister's visit. "People in Greece know what's happening and people in Turkey know what's happening and still every day boats are coming across and people are dying," she said. "It doesn't make any sense."

Ruby Brookman Prins, 19, said conditions were so desperate at Moria that some refugees had asked them how they could return home. "They don't want to be here, they just want to leave," she said: "They say this is as bad as Syria, but without the bombs. They don't expect this in Europe."

Even as the leaders visited, families were walking around with limp children in their arms desperately searching for doctors, picking over rubbish and gullies running with raw sewerage. "We need a doctor," one woman from Afghanistan said. "My baby is sick, if she stays outside for one more night she will die."

Aid workers say conditions at Moria, which is for non-Syrians, have dramatically improved over the past month with the arrival of more agencies and the construction of cabins to house refugees. The camp is overflowing, with hundreds of families with babies and young children sleeping in flimsy tents or without shelter on rocky ground.

At least 430 people have died this year trying to make the short sea crossing along Greece's border with Turkey. Mr Tsipras said it was "imperative" to reach a deal with Ankara to stem the flow. Some 15,000 refugees and migrants were effectively stranded on Lesbos because a ferry strike had stopped reception centres forwarding arrivals onto the Greek mainland. "It's an asphyxiating situation," Mr Tsipras said.

Together with Mr Schulz, Mr Tsipras visited a new accommodation block planned at Moria. One man shouted at Mr Tsipras: "We are here three days. We are hungry. I have two children, my children are sick." "We will do our best," the Prime Minister responded.

Elsewhere in the camp, hundreds of people queued for registration papers and unaccompanied teenagers were siphoned off to a former detention centre surrounded by barbed wire. Parts of Lesbos have been designated "hotspots", from where European nations who have pledged to take migrants from within Europe can transfer them. But several nations, including the UK, have opted out.

In Molyvos, on the Greek island's north coast, the beaches have become almost buried under sunken dinghies, inflatibles, clothes, shoes and detritus left by desperate rescue operations.

The United Nations refugee agency UNHCR launched a new funding appeal yesterday, saying it needed £63m in additional support for Greece and affected Balkan countries.

Lizzie Dearden

9 November 2015
FEAR TERRORISTS USING REFUGEE CRISIS CONFIRMED

Fears that Islamic terror groups might be entering Europe on refugee boats appear to have been confirmed after police in Sicily identified a convicted terrorist among asylum-seekers arriving from Libya. The Tunisian, Ben Nasr Mehdi, was first arrested in Italy in November 2007 and sentenced to seven years for planning terror attacks for a group that has since been linked to Isis. After his release from the high-security Benevento prison in southern Italy, he was expelled from the country.

But it has emerged that he has attempted to enter Italy again, following his arrest last month by Italian authorities after arriving at the island of Lampedusa, off Sicily. He was among 200 refugees rescued at sea by a navy vessel on 4 October.

Despite giving a false name and claiming that he was seeking asylum in northern Europe to escape political persecution, finger prints revealed his true identity. He was held along with three other men, thought to be the human traffickers who had organised the trip, and interrogated by police in the Sicilian city of Agrigento.

Several days later Mehdi, 38, was repatriated, and put into the hands of Tunisian authorities. Local press reports suggest that authorities had attempted to conceal the incident to prevent panic.

Italy's Interior Minister, Angelino Alfano, had previously insisted there was no evidence that Islamic terrorists were sneaking into Europe aboard refugee boats, despite warnings from right-of-centre politicians that the wave of migration from North Africa represented a serious security threat. Mr Alfano, has said however, that Italian security forces are constantly looking out for such a threat.

The interior ministry was not able to respond to The Independent's request for comment yesterday. Italian authorities have said, however, they regard Mehdi as one of the most dangerous terrorists to have operated in Italy. He is considered to be an explosives expert and a contact for organisations that recruit jihadists from Syria, Iraq and Afghanistan.

Upon his arrest seven years ago, in Novellara, northern Italy, police said they had seized poisons, remote explosive detonators and manuals on guerrilla warfare. He was captured then along with 13 Algerians and Tunisians across Europe as part of an anti-terrorism operation led by Italian authorities. Medhi's seven year sentence, based largely on 25 wiretaps, was confirmed by the Reggio Emilia appeal court in 2011.

The operation was ordered by Milan prosecutors and targeted northern Italian cities as well as Britain, France and Portugal. Investigators said the group had been setting up "Salafist jihadi" militant cells that had recruited and assisted would-be suicide bombers in Iraq and Afghanistan.

A few days before his arrest, Mehdi, who was working as a bricklayer, was wiretapped talking to terrorists in Damascus, prosecutors said. The recording suggested he supplied them instructions and contacts, thus indicating his senior role in the organisation. Italian prosecutors said that Mehdi's principal terror activity was organising attacks in the Middle East.

In May this year, however, an adviser to the Libyan government based in Tobruk told the BBC that Isis fighters were being smuggled into Europe by gangs in the Mediterranean. The official, Abdul Basit Haroun, based his claim on conversations with smugglers in parts of North Africa controlled by militants. Some senior military officials, including Nato Secretary-General Jens Stoltenberg, have expressed similar fears.

Michael Day

10 November 2015
EUROPE'S REFUGEE FAILURE

European leaders gathering in Malta tomorrow for a two day summit with their African counterparts are expected to announce a scheme to manage migration involving billions of euros in aid. However, for all their pledges, European governments have fallen woefully short of meeting their own targets to tackle the crisis.

This winter, hundreds of thousands of men, women and children could risk the migrant routes from Italy and Greece through the Balkans to countries such as Germany and Sweden. Charities and officials have warned that as temperatures drop, they cannot guarantee their safety. But although the Malta meeting is the sixth time this year that EU leaders will address the migration crisis, governments are still unable to provide the money, manpower and resources to prevent a humanitarian catastrophe over the next few weeks. The challenge was underlined last week when the European Commission said it expected three million migrants to arrive in Europe by 2017.

"European leaders keep agreeing measures that are too little and too late," said John Dalhuisen, Amnesty International's Europe director. "There is a glaring lack of leadership, vision and solidarity.

For all the rhetoric about restricting migration, the numbers will keep coming."

Despite a series of acrimonious, late-night summits, and an ambitious programme of policies to try to solve the refugee crisis, national governments have so far failed to live up to their promises. When it comes to relocation, which involves redistributing migrants across the EU, progress has been almost absurdly slow: only 105 refugees out of 39,600 pledged from Italy, and 30 out of 66,400 from Greece. Since most border policies are national prerogatives, the EU institutions have pleaded with capitals to act, and will do so again in Malta. "This crisis is exploding in our faces," said Camino Mortera-Martinez, a research fellow at the Londonbased Centre for European Reform (CER). "The main problem is that we don't have a common approach."

The meeting with African leaders will be followed, on Thursday, by a hastily arranged internal summit of the EU's 28 leaders, which will look at how to manage the flow of people while keeping Europe's visa-free Schengen zone. Since the latest surge of refugees this summer, member states including Hungary have erected razor-wire border fences with non-Schengen members.

European Council President Donald Tusk, who chairs the EU summits, and European Commission President Jean-Claude Juncker, along with Luxembourg Prime Minister Xavier Bettel - which holds the EU's rotating presidency - will call out national capitals for not doing what they promised in providing money and resources to secure borders, process asylum claims and fund development programmes. "As I have warned before, the only way not to dismantle Schengen is to ensure proper management of EU external borders," Mr Tusk said in his summit invitation letter to EU leaders. The British Labour MEP Claude Moraes, who chairs the European Parliament's Civil Liberties Committee, blamed national governments for the chaotic response to the crisis. "This is an indictment of EU member states, who have only been looking at this from a domestic political point of view," he said.

Mr Moraes said that since the EU itself does not yet have the resources to manage the crisis, the onus is on national governments. "Only national governments have the navies, military resources, and emergency services - the major assets that rescue, help, redistribute people," he said. "But they are simply in denial. They will not do the work."

One of the main points of the summit in Valletta, Malta's capital, is for the EU to push reluctant African leaders to help by offering them development aid in exchange for taking back economic migrants. The aid will tackle what the EU sees as the root causes of migration for Africans, who account for around a quarter of the nearly 800,000 migrants who have landed on European shores this year. But even on this, EU governments have been unable to find the money they have promised: the €1.8bn Emergency Trust Fund has so far only generated €47.5m in contributions from EU member state coffers.

The draft EU summit plan identifies wars and poverty in Africa, as well as Islamic radicalisation, for instance, in Nigeria with the Boko Haram group, as key drivers for migration. It outlines new measures to resolve conflicts, such as those in Libya and the regions of Sahel, Lake Chad and the Horn of Africa. But the plan suggests that most migrants leaving Africa are looking for work and do not qualify for asylum, so it includes arrangements to send them back.

It also opens legal channels for a limited number of others - students, researchers and entrepreneurs - to enter the EU legally. "Rekindling hope, notably for the African youth, must be our paramount objective," the draft summit conclusions say, while noting that, "efforts should be made to advance legal migration and mobility possibilities."

Leo Cendrowicz

16 November 2015

REFUGEE CRISIS PART OF ISIS PROPAGANDA WAR

The Syrian passport found near the remains of a suicide bomber at the Stade de France intrigues French investigators for many reasons.

"The single most intriguing fact is that the passport was there at all," one French official source said yesterday. "It was not actually on the terrorist's body, or what remained of it. It was lying nearby, as if meant to be found." The holder of the passport was named yesterday as Ahmed Almuhamed, aged 25. A man of this name entered the European Union on a Syrian passport with 69 other refugees after their boat sank off the Greek island of Leros on 3 October.

The idea that one of the Paris "black Friday" terrorists may have been a recent Syrian refugee to the EU was seized upon gleefully by right-wing newspapers and politicians across Europe yesterday. The discovery appeared to substantiate claims that Isis terrorists have infiltrated the hundreds of thousands of refugees who have entered Europe this year.

French officials say that they have no proof that the Stade de France suicide bomber - one of three who detonated crude explosive belts at the stadium - was Mr Almuhamed. Intelligence sources in the US told CBS news that there are doubts whether the passport is authentic. The number of the document is incorrect and name does not match the picture, it was claimed.

Paris police were reported to have believed that the passport, and another found at the scene, were fakes made in Turkey. There is known to be a flourishing trade in fake Syrian passports in both Turkey and Europe. But that does not necessarily mean that the man who entered Greece as a refugee was not also the man who blew himself up.

French investigators fear that the apparent "planting" of the passport is part of a sophisticated propaganda war being waged by Isis. "There are three possibilities," one source said. "He is the man whose name is on the passport. He was a false refugee, travelling on a false passport. Or he is someone else and a false passport was deliberately left there to sow confusion."

In all three cases, Isis appears to have set out to stoke popular anger against Syrian migrants as part of their campaign to foment anti-Muslim feeling. The man travelling as Mr Almuhamed entered Greece with another man called Mohamed Almuhamed, who was presumed to be his brother. Ahmed then turned up, Serbian authorities said yesterday, at a Macedonian border crossing four days later.

A spokeswoman for the Croatian Interior Ministry said the man was registered at the Opatovac refugee camp on 8 October and crossed into Hungary, making for Austria. Austrian officials insisted yesterday that there was no record of him.

Ursula von der Leyen, Germany's Defence Minister, appeared to doubt that Mr Almuhamed, whoever he may be, had taken part in the attack. She said linking the refugee crisis to the threat of terrorism would be wrong. "Terrorism is so well organised that it doesn't have to risk the sometimes lifethreatening crossings at sea."

John Lichfield

20 November 2015

PARIS CHANGED EVERYTHING FOR MERKEL

It was hardly an auspicious beginning to the week leading up to this Sunday's tenth anniversary of Angela Merkel's taking office, when the politician's admirers will quietly celebrate a decade of her uninterrupted reign as German Chancellor, if not "Queen of Europe".

For a few tense hours on Tuesday her intelligence services became convinced the terror of Paris was about to spread to Germany, and that the Chancellor was a target.

The warning came as Merkel sat in a plane on her way to Hanover, where she had been due to watch a Germany-Holland friendly football match. The game was supposed to be a gesture of public defiance against the terrorists who committed the atrocities in France, and Merkel was due to meet the German team - who had the previous Friday been forced to spend the night in the Stade de France after the suicide bombers' attacks.

Now, German intelligence warned, terrorists planned to smuggle explosives into the Hanover soccer stadium in an ambulance and detonate several bombs. The ringleader planned to film the attack. Merkel took her Interior Minister's advice and cancelled the match before flying back to Berlin. In a statement later she said she "was sure" cancelling the game was the right decision.

In the event, police failed to find any explosives in or around Hanover. Yet Germany's security services remain on high alert and continue to speak of the "serious terrorist threat" facing the country. Tensions in Germany have been further heightened by reports that one of the Isis terrorists who attacked the French capital had entered Europe from Syria, posing as a refugee.

In Germany such reports inevitably put the spotlight on Merkel's controversial "open-door" policy, which is expected to result in an influx of well over one million refugees from Syria, Afghanistan and Iraq this year alone. Even before Paris, Merkel faced mounting public discontent and growing rebellion over the issue from within the ranks of her own Christian Democrats, with MPs demanding that Germany halt the "uncontrolled influx" by closing its eastern borders.

The Paris attacks have exacerbated Merkel's problems, prompting demands that the German army be deployed along the country's borders for the first time in several decades. "Paris has changed everything," insisted Marcus Söder, a leading member of the Bavarian sister party to the Chancellor's Christian Democrats, which has been highly critical of her refugee policies. Söder and other senior conservatives in Berlin are currently demanding that Germany regain the ability to close its borders. "If we don't then voters will lose their confidence in the Chancellor," warned the Christian Democrat MP Klaus Peter-Willsch last week. It was the first time since the beginning of Germany's refugee crisis in September that one of Merkel's MPs has openly suggested that the Chancellor risks being ousted by voters if she persists with her controversial stance.

Yet his remarks were merely the tip of an iceberg of opposition that Merkel now faces. Opinion polls show that a majority of Germans are unhappy with her refugee policies. The number of far right attacks on asylum homes and individual refugees has topped 500 this year. Merkel's conservative party grass roots are up in arms; at a meeting of the party faithful in the east German town of Schkeuditz last month she was confronted with placards that read "Stop the refugee chaos" and "Dethrone Merkel".

Opinion polls show that Germany's new and increasingly xenophobic Alternative für Deutschland party could win as much as 10 per cent of the vote nationally. Such an outcome would make it Germany's third-main political party. In the meantime, to Germany's dismay, the European Union has done little to help share the refugee burden.

Yet Merkel has doggedly refused to consider an upper limit to the number of refugees Germany is prepared to accept, and continues to insist: "Wir schaffen das" - "We can do it". Merkel now faces the most difficult challenge of her 10 years as Chancellor. One of the few safeguards against her being ousted from power is the absence of any rival political figure with the stature needed to replace her. She has made sure of that.

But her open-door refugee policy itself represented a formidable U-turn by Merkel. As recently as July she was castigated for reducing a teenage Palestinian girl to tears after telling her she could not stay in Germany. "If I say you can all come and you all come - we just can't manage that," the Chancellor insisted.

What induced Merkel to change her mind? Sources within her government say the dramatically growing volume of refugees heading for Europe this summer was one factor. Another was that with one of the lowest birth rates in the world, 600,000 job vacancies and a booming economy, Germany could not only cope with an influx of mostly educated refugees from countries like Syria - it also needed them.

But earlier this month Merkel put forward another, perhaps more convincing, argument. She told party members that if Germany were to close its doors to the refugee tide, it would trigger a chain reaction in an already volatile Balkan region that could lead to war. "I don't want there to be another military confrontation down there," she insisted.

Seasoned Merkel observers such as the Berlin politics professor Herfried Münkler say that she opened the door to refugees "without a plan". She now faces a divided government and forces within it bent on stopping the refugee influx. The odds seem stacked against her. Her future as Chancellor will depend on her ability to defeat her critics both in Germany and Europe by turning a refugee "crisis" into a success story. Not a few say that this time, Angela Merkel may have bitten off more than even she can chew.

Tony Paterson

December 2015

WELCOME TO THE FRONTIER OF EUROPE

Samos, Greece with Turkish coast in background, 12 October 2015

5 December 2015

'THE GUANTANAMO OF SAMOS'

Mohammad Raza's view from the hill high above Samos town is spectacular, the horseshoe bay and glistening blue water which feature on hundreds of postcards sold in the local tourist shops dotted around the cobbled streets below.

The 15-year-old Afghan's immediate surroundings, however, couldn't be more different, a high barb wiretopped fence encircling the so-called "reception centre" where thousands of migrants end up if they survive the perilous eight-mile boat trip from Turkey to Greece, to escape war and persecution and to find work.

Welcome to the frontier of Europe, or as one local activist calls it "the Guantanamo of Samos". Mohammad's eyes redden as he tells how his father, a farmer, is still waiting for papers so they can leave the island and continue their journey towards Sweden, 11 days after they were rescued from a dinghy.

"My brother and I have got our papers, but my father hasn't. Why? We have done our fingerprints two weeks ago but no answer yet. Every day I go there and they just say 'No, no, no, we don't know anything.'" His family fled fighting and extreme poverty in Afghanistan and hoped to make a new life in Pakistan.

But they could not pay for education there, and so Mohammad's father took him and his 12-year-old brother to Turkey, leaving behind his wife and daughter, in the hope they could make a living in Europe. "We had no money. We were forced to leave our country. Isis slaughtered our brothers and sisters." Stuck in this limbo, Mohammad survives mostly with food given out by local and international volunteers.

His anger is shared by Chris Jones, 64, a retired professor of sociology at the University of Liverpool, who lives a few hundred yards from the camp and dedicates his time to helping the migrants. "It's styled on Guantanamo, it opened in around 2007 and they spent 13 million euros on it. They said it was an example of Greeks' hospitality towards the refugees. It was a closed camp. Everyone who came to the island was arrested, put inside and the normal stay until a year ago was 30 days, and for unaccompanied minors three or four months.

"It was locked, nobody was allowed in and nobody allowed out. They didn't want any of the refugees to be seen in the town. Now of course with the thousands who have come they are in the town, you can't avoid it. It's run by the police according to prison rules, and opened about a month ago because they couldn't feed them. They said to the refugees, 'We can't do anything, go, go, find food." The crisis peaked in the summer and spiked again last month when a weeklong ferry strike meant 6,000 migrants and refugees were on the island. Rough weather and Turkey's new crackdown on the smugglers has reduced the number, but calm seas this week have brought another 600 to Samos, nearly half from Syria. "It was incredible, we saw nobody -- no MSF, no Save the Children, nothing. All the work was done by the volunteers," said Mr Jones.

"All the charities have come in November, and my first question to them was, 'Where have you been?'" The camp is currently home to about 300 people from Afghanistan, Iran, Iraq and elsewhere waiting to be processed by the Greek police so that they can continue north to claim asylum mostly in Germany, Sweden or Austria.

Syrians with passports are given priority and needn't leave the port, where they are usually fingerprinted and given permission to buy a ferry ticket to Athens and travel within a day or two.

Greece has long had to deal with waves of migration but this year's crisis is off the scale, with more than 600,000 people arriving along its maritime border so far. In Samos, about 98,000 have come, more than three times the island's population. The challenge for the local authorities to police these hundreds of islands is huge, with the eyes of increasingly wary European nations on Greece in the wake of the Paris attacks.

Many migrants arrive without documentation and it is the task of the island's 120-strong police force, with the help of other agencies, to contact the relevant embassies and establish who they are. Frontex, the EU's border agency, has sent 190 screeners, fingerprint officers and other experts to help the Greeks.

They have asked for 600 more, but the rest of the EU have agreed to only about half that number. The island's chief of police, Superintendent Evagelos Tsirigos, insists the processing of so many migrants has been "smooth" but admits the crisis has forced other areas of policing to be sacrificed.

He said: "We have to drop lots of things and work 24/7 to maintain a smooth process for everybody. It's been really hard but we haven't had the same numbers (of migrants) as Lesbos." Hearteningly, hardly any crime has been committed by the migrants. "All they want is food, clothes, and shelter. And they're grateful when they get it," said one officer.

It is not only the living whom Samos are coping with. This year more than 50 dead migrants have had to be recovered from the local waters and coastline. The unenviable job of photographing and identifying them falls to the island's only police forensics officer, George Antoniadis -- aka "CSI Samos".

He told how two weeks ago the uncle of a migrant who died last year travelled from the US to give fingerprints in the hope he can still be identified. The young man has long since been buried but Mr Antoniadis and his colleagues do everything they can identify those who drown trying to reach freedom. "We don't just dump them in a landfill or somewhere. We try to treat everybody with the respect they deserve."

But among the suffering can be found stories of hope. On Tuesday a pregnant woman from Syria arrived. Almost as soon as she stepped ashore she felt terrible pains and was taken to hospital where she delivered a healthy baby.

Michael Howie

7 December 2015

'THE COAST OF DEATH'

Something in the water, 11 o'clock," cries Jens. The lifeboat suddenly thrusts into life, picking up speed as it arcs through the sea towards the bright orange object. This time it isn't a person, only a discarded lifejacket -- one of thousands dotted around this jewel in the Aegean Sea that is at the epicentre of possibly Europe's worst migration crisis since the Second World War.

We zip out along the eastern coast of Samos, towards the towering 500 foot cliffs on wild Cape Praso.

From the coast of Turkey, clearly visible just a few miles away, it must seem tantalisingly close. But it is along this rugged stretch that the migrants, squeezed by the dozen into their flimsy dinghies, least want to land.

"We call it the coast of death," says Jens Samuelsson, one of a team of volunteers from the Swedish Sea Rescue Society -- similar to Britain's RNLI --who have come to help the Hellenic Coast Guard with migrant rescues. "The only way out is up those towering cliffs, and there are no roads leading you to safety. I'm amazed anyone survives."

Two weeks ago the crew were called to rescue 19 migrants who had managed to clamber 50 metres up onto a ledge. They were stuck on the cliff for about 12 hours, some with mild hypothermia, all terrified, hungry and dehydrated. Half were children and one was elderly.

"We carried all the children and lowered one of the crew by ropes down the cliff. It was extremely challenging," said the full-time helicopter winch-man. The Swedes are among a number of dedicated volunteers on Samos -- international and local --who have responded to the humanitarian crisis. One of the toughest jobs is done by a team of divers from a local club, who last month had to recover the bodies of 11 women and children trapped inside a migrant boat as it sank only 25 metres from the coast.

"We entered the cabin and found the bodies of the refugees. Six of them were children," says Alexandros Malagaris, president of the Samos Divers Association.

Last year, the bodies of 18 migrants had to be pulled from another capsized boat. Mr Malagaris added: "We went in thinking we'd find three or four bodies. What we encountered was terrible, it was like a puzzle of humanity, legs, arms intertwined."

The Greek people's response to the crisis on Samos -- where 98,000 migrants and refugees have arrived this year -- is truly inspirational.

Every day Iokasti Nikolaidi prepares hundreds of meals to hand out to refugees and migrants, many of whom have no money. The mother of-four, 41, started buying cookies and croissants to give out, but as the arrivals grew she realised a bigger effort was needed. Now she and 25 other women from the villages prepare hundreds of meals a day. They often dip into their own pockets to buy the produce.

"We couldn't keep giving them cookies so I thought, 'We need to cook food, with oil, with tomatoes.' It started with 100, then became 200, 300... a few weeks ago we were making 5,000 meals!" said Ms Nikolaidi.

Down at the port, where the new arrivals are processed, Elena Housni sorts out bags of clothes, shoes, blankets and rucksacks donated by people in Britain.

The former journalist, 42, has thrown herself into the humanitarian effort, single-handedly organising a squad of dedicated but untrained volunteers who come from across Europe -- including some from London -- to provide the often desperate refugees with basic items they need to survive. Every evening, at 8pm, the volunteers distribute clothes. With winter setting in, many refugees arrive with no shoes and simply need to be kept warm. It's a tough, time consuming job getting people into a line and attending to their needs one by one -- little children in need of gloves, a scarf and a smile.

Meanwhile, a small group of volunteers from Switzerland prepare huge vats of soup to ensure everyone has something warm inside them as night approaches.

"Our dream is not just to give to those people food and the cover they need, our dream is for Samos to become the role model for refugees in Europe," said Ms Housni.

"We want to be the best, not for us but for them. We want to show Europe that these are people who really need help. They've experienced the worst things that can happen to somebody -- war, they've lost everything, they've lost their houses, their jobs, their country.

"They come here and we see how grateful they are. It's wonderful, they are giving us lessons every day."

Michael Howie

17 December 2015

MOST BRITONS WOULD NOT OFFER REFUGEES A ROOM

People in the UK are among the least welcoming in Europe towards refugees, according to a survey of opinion in 14 countries.

Only 20 per cent of Britons would be willing to house a refugee in their home for a short period if they had a spare room, while 80 per cent would refuse entirely. Of the countries surveyed by ORB International, only Bulgaria, which has adopted a hard line in the migration crisis, had a lower score, with 14 per cent of people saying they would offer a refugee a place in their home.

The most welcoming nation is Spain, where 62 per cent of people said they would open their door to a refugee if they had a spare room. In Germany - which is due to accept one million refugees this year - and Greece, the figure was 48 per cent.

The UK was well below the 35 per cent average of the 14 countries surveyed. ORB International questioned 1,000 people in England, Scotland and Wales as part of a poll of 13,800 adults across Europe.

Johnny Heald, its managing director, said: "It is hardly a good advert for the Big Society."

When Britain tries to win a new European deal, it has to negotiate with 27 other EU member states. Leo Cendrowicz and Oliver Wright assess the attitudes of some of the leaders David Cameron will speak to:

Angela Merkel, Germany

Europe's matriarch usually sets the tone for summits, calmly ushering fellow leaders towards her position. She has long argued that the EU must do what it can to keep the UK inside but has her limits, and curbs to free movement are a non-starter.

François Hollande, France

He has become more concerned in recent months about Brexit prospects, with far-right leader Marine Le Pen making ever louder calls for a similar referendum in France. While he is wary of a special deal to protect UK financial services, he backs initiatives to reduce bureaucracy.

Matteo Renzi, Italy

Mr Renzi has a youthful, centrist dynamism similar to Mr Cameron's, and his efforts to reform the Italian economy echo the renegotiation demands about European competitiveness. However, with Italy currently straining under the refugee crisis, Mr Renzi may baulk at Mr Cameron's hostility to migrants.

Mark Rutte, Netherlands

Mr Rutte is a close Cameron ally in the EU and often sounds exactly like the Prime Minister when cautioning against red tape from Brussels. Expect his vocal support.

Mariano Rajoy, Spain

Spanish voters go to the polls on Sunday, and if Mr Rajoy is still in office when the talks conclude next year, he is expected to oppose the "red card" for national parliaments.

António Costa, Portugal

Mr Costa has been in office less than a month and this is his first EU summit. His Socialistled government, backed by radical left-wing parties, is less supportive of Mr Cameron's open-market initiatives, and his planned restrictions on migrants' access to welfare.

Charles Michel and Xavier Bettel, Belgium and Luxembourg

Perhaps the most federalist EU leaders, they have an emotional attachment to integration and will resist moves to weaken "ever-closer union", but are still likely to accept a compromise.

Enda Kenny, Ireland

Mr Kenny knows Ireland is the EU state with most at risk from a British exit: he may be the most helpful leader throughout the renegotiation.

Viktor Orbán, Hungary

Mr Orbán will support Mr Cameron's proposals to give greater powers to national parliaments and protect countries not in the eurozone. But limiting migrant benefits is a red line.

Beata Szydlo, Poland

Ideologically close to the Tories, she will back three of Mr Cameron's four reform "pillars". But with Poles making up the single-largest group of migrants to Britain she cannot give ground on benefit restrictions.

Poll results

Q If you were asked to and had a spare room in your house, would you be willing to house a refugee for a short period while their paperwork was being finalised?

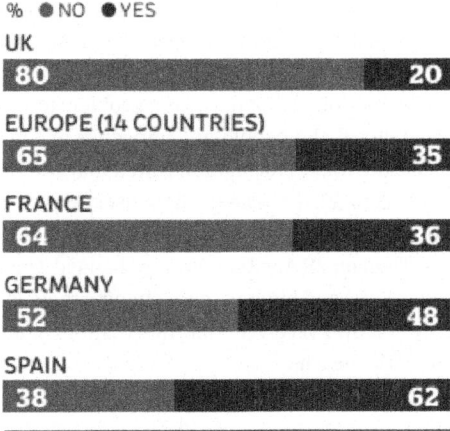

% ● NO ● YES

UK
80 | 20

EUROPE (14 COUNTRIES)
65 | 35

FRANCE
64 | 36

GERMANY
52 | 48

SPAIN
38 | 62

SOURCE: ORB/THE INDEPENDENT

Andrew Grice

23 December 2015

ONE MILLION AND COUNTING

More than one million people have arrived in Europe by irregular means this year, the International Organisation for Migration announced, in the biggest wave of mass migration in Europe since the aftermath of the Second World War.

Reporting a total of 1,005,504 arrivals by 21 December, the IOM said that the great majority - more than 800,000 - entered by sea into Greece.

It is the issue that has defined 2015 more than any other. And as the year draws to a close, there is little sign that Europe is getting nearer to resolving it in a decent manner. The moments of unanimity and accord have been rare.

Yet Europe cannot say it was not warned: the refugee crisis has been under way for decades. Every year, many hundreds have died trying to reach the European Union from the north coast of Africa. Europe turned to look, uttered words of concern, and went back to business.

Then the Syrian civil war broke out and, as it grew more and more destructive, refugees fled in their millions to Jordan, Lebanon and Turkey. Some reached the North African coast: Muammar Gaddafi, who had cynically turned the refugee tap on and off to suit his own purposes, was gone, and the pitiful boats tossed on the waves of the Strait of Sicily multiplied. But this was a problem for the bereaved, the Sicilian coast guard, the people of Lampedusa or the Italian government, because the Dublin Regulation stated that where an asylum-seeker first made landfall, there he or she must seek asylum.

It was not a problem for the rest of Europe - not one that demanded action. Then on 28 April something changed. On the island of Lesbos, Dimitrios Vatis and his staff were opening their seafront hotel for the season when they received their first visitors: not through the front door but on the beach.

"This was a small boat, with just 15 people on board," said Mr Vatis's daughter, Aphrodite. "There were kids on the boat, they handed them over to us. They were all wet and cold, so we opened rooms in the hotel for them and made them comfortable.

"I went home and got some of my children's clothes, and we dried them and dressed them and soon they were running around. It's hard to see these children in your own clothes - it's a strange feeling."

The Libyan coast is 180 miles of rough, open sea from Lampedusa. The crossing, in a leaky, overcrowded hulk, is mortally risky. Turkey, by contrast, is only five miles from the north coast of Lesbos. From the island's tourist town of Molyvos, the Turkish shore is plainly visible. Boats with refugees have always come across, says Eric Kempson, an Englishman who has lived there for 16 years. "In the past there would be one or two boats a week," he says.

But suddenly the numbers exploded. By September, 3,000 people were arriving every day. The population of the "nation of the displaced" - the world's refugees - surged by many millions in 2014, and now, thanks to this quick and relatively easy passage, a fair fraction were heading our way. The IOM reports that Lesbos is now Europe's principal informal gateway. Europe found itself woefully unprepared for what its leaders euphemistically called "the challenge of the migrant influx". The Dublin Regulation ensured that frontline states bore the brunt of arrivals. That bred complacency in the rest of the union. Europe's maritime borders were essentially undefended, the responsibility of an EU agency called Frontex, which had neither the budget nor capacity to fulfil its role: nothing impeded the people-smugglers. A continent without borders was part of EU holy writ. So Europe woke up to find tens, then hundreds of thousands spilling across the continent towards the affluent parts - Germany and Scandinavia - believed most likely to make them welcome.

Politically speaking, a refugee crisis is a dead loss. The only parties to benefit are jingoists who exploit it to whip up popular paranoia. Leaders who want to do the right thing are hamstrung by the fact that it can only leave them less popular than before. That may explain why Europe has been so apathetic.

But then on 2 September a three-year-old boy called Aylan Kurdi slipped from his father's arms as the rubber boat in which they were crossing from Turkey capsized. Later his lifeless body, face down in the sand, was photographed: the image went around the world, and that single picture transformed the way the crisis was understood. Suddenly the "barbarian armies" became what they actually were - a flock of desperate people who had lost their homes and now risked losing their lives.

The reaction was instantaneous. German Chancellor Angela Merkel declared the Dublin Regulation suspended, which meant that those landing in Lesbos could now legitimately dream of Berlin; she confirmed this by saying she expected Germany to take 800,000 refugees. And the rest of Europe echoed her compassion. "Refugees welcome" placards were everywhere. Even David Cameron, safely outside the Schengen zone, declared himself "deeply shocked" by Aylan's pitiful image and Britain agreed to admit 20,000, spread over five years. The crisis briefly became a feel-good story.

Today, that period looks like a delusive blip. What happened next was that Europe discovered it was not one, but two: the eastern parts, including Hungary, Serbia and Croatia, remembered their centuries under the Ottoman boot, the escape from which defined their modern identities. As Ms Merkel was promising to redeem German's modern history by welcoming all comers, the continent's eastern marches were haunted by older ghosts, bolstering chauvinists such as Hungary's Prime Minister, Viktor Orban. Suddenly Europe's dreams of abolishing borders evaporated as fences and walls were rushed up.

Large though Europe's inflows are, they are dwarfed by the grand total of the displaced worldwide: 13.9 million in 2014, according to the United Nations High Commissioner For Refugees, the vast number accommodated - with little fuss - by countries far poorer than any in the EU. That's the measure of Europe's shame.

Peter Popham

24 December 2015

ISIS PROFITING FROM THE REFUGEES

With the upsurge of fighting in Afghanistan, and the continued menace of Islamic State in four or more main battle areas, not to forget the continuous conflict in Yemen and many parts of east and central Africa, there is not much sense that peace will break out in the new year.

IS as an organization and idea is evolving new strategies and ways of making money, principally in taking over the refugee and migrant operations in the Mediterranean, Iraq, Syria and Afghanistan.

It has been winning recruits from old Taliban organisations in Afghanistan and is now believed to be promoting the outflow of migrants from big cities like Kabul, with traffickers under their control.

"IS operates strategically. It is interested in taking and holding territory, and managing revenue streams far more than is generally realised," says Professor Jonathan Githens-Mazer, of Exeter University, who has just returned from a study tour of Libya and Tunisia. "Owning territory is an important credential, and I think IS is now preparing a major sweep west from Libya. I think they will move on Tunisia, and establish their capital in the old religious centre of Kairouan. This all makes Libya a much more serious priority since I estimate the encirclement of IS in Syria is now only a matter of time."

Two peace agreements for Libya and for an interim government for Syria have been sponsored by the UN in the past month. In the case of Syria the plan has been enshrined by a Security Council Resolution.

But both plans have obvious weaknesses. The one for Syria does not state what should happen to President Assad and his entourage in a final peace deal. The Assad regime is directly responsible for the flight of more Syrian refugees than IS. The regime has neither the credibility nor force to rule the whole of Syria as it once did, and to the range of opposition forces, however moderate some may be, the Assad-Alawite brand is toxic.

Credible ground forces will have to take and hold the lands recovered from IS, and it is hard to see how this can be done without outside help and management, and command and control by international forces of Nato standard. The Saudi proposal for a 34 Islamic nation force to defeat IS lacks military credibility.

Despite the increased tempo of bombing since last month's devastating commando-terrorist attacks in Paris, IS still manages to draw recruits from across Europe and Asia. The social media narrative is as powerful as ever.

In Libya, IS has established a new capital, with instruments of government, in Sirte. Thousands of fighters have been rallying there, according to Professor Githens-Mazer, 2,500 from Tunisia alone.

Local Libyans have rejected IS and its hierarchy in Sirte is made up of recruits from Iraq, Yemen, Bahrain, Syria and Lebanon. The trafficking of migrants across the Mediterranean has shown no sign of slackening in the stormy winter months. The European naval task force picked up nearly 5,000 drowning migrants from the sea in one week alone at the beginning of this month.

Italy in particular is desperate to mount an operation against IS in Libya. This would support a new unity government agreed for Libya earlier this month. It combines the two main ruling factions and armies from Benghazi and Tripoli. They are the best armed and equipped formations in Libya, but there are more than 300 militias at large who will be reluctant to lay down their arms.

The UK Government has been briefing that it would be prepared to commit 1,000 military personnel to a coalition force led by the Italians. As ever, journalists were assured that this doesn't mean "boots on the ground", whatever that means in this case. David Cameron seems to be indulging in his belief in "Intervention Lite" which risks being as dangerous as no intervention at all.

President Obama is against any serious US ground commitment. In a background briefing to journalists last week he said that he would not commit ground troops to the Middle East "at the risk of 500 lives a month". It was like Bismarck declaring in the 1870s the Balkans not being "worth the bones of a single Pomeranian grenadier". Mr Obama's briefing, which went viral, was the clearest declaration by a US president of a lack of commitment to a global crisis, afflicting allies and US interests, of our times. At the heart of that crisis is IS.

Joan Smith

29 December 2015

SYRIA'S WAR IS COMPLEX – OFFERING REFUGE IS NOT

There was a time when I would find "it's complicated" to be a mildly aggravating response to troubles in the Middle East. That was when the phrase was most popularly applied to the Israeli-Palestinian conflict, and it felt lazy because actually that conflict is relatively straightforward (you know the script: two states, 1967 borders, Jerusalem as a shared capital) and could be resolved if there was a political will or sufficient pressure to do so. Now, however, it's the opposite urge - to oversimplify the complex, horrendous war in Syria - that is becoming so unhelpfully prevalent and annoying.

Such tendencies were on full display during the political debate over British air strikes in Syria, which Parliament approved at the beginning of December. Yes, we understand why the "villains and heroes" narrative so crudely trotted out during these endless "war on terror" years has been appealing when making a case for intervention. Yes, in the face of Isis's murderous actions, the blood-curdling atrocities and appalling apocalyptic zeal, "bomb them" has an edifying ring to it. And, yes, the hand-wringing cry of every Western liberal interventionist to "do something" to help (as though the choice is to bomb or to do nothing, as though we were not already and unhelpfully meddling in Syria) is reliant on a certain oversimplification.

But trying to find, or suggest that it is even possible to find, easy answers or explanations for the gruesome Syrian war does nothing but serve our own sense of self-importance and a prevailing British impetus to be relevant in the world.

The alternative perspective, however, would mean taking a hard look at what our meddling has done so far, and just how long it would

take to reverse ravaging effects played out over decades. It would require honesty about the impact of the Iraq war: how the consequent,
and foretold, decimation of that country furrowed the ground on
which Isis now thrives.

More than that, it would mean examining the decades of support
for brutal dictatorships in the Middle East, support for regimes that
have crushed any nascent democratic movements, contributing to the
lack of significant secular, progressive opposition forces today. We
would also have to be honest about the activities of our allies: how far
have countries such as Turkey, Saudi Arabia and other Gulf states contributed to the rise of Isis and other violent jihadi groups? It would
mean taking seriously the question of what happens if and when Isis
is routed from its current strongholds: how to ensure this group, or
worse, cannot take hold again. And we would have to be brutally honest about the need to properly engage with perceived "enemies" -
Russia and Iran - over Syria, because that is critical to any lasting resolution to the war.

But while the war and its causes may be complicated, other big
issues facing us are still fairly straightforward - far more so than we
make out. The refugee crisis precipitated by this bloody war is one of
them.

We've let the European Union obfuscate, peddling tedious bureaucracy over who should be allowed across which border and under
what terms. How is it that Lebanon and Jordan - smaller, less wealthy
nations - are able to take in more refugees than the whole of Europe
put together? Turkey has more than two million refugees from Syria,
Jordan is home to 1.5 million and Lebanon to more than one million,
comprising one fifth of its total population.

The harsh reality is that the EU is not adequately responding to
the refugee crisis because many of its member states (the UK included) don't want it to. The European response has been less about
what could be done to help people fleeing war, and more a self-ab-
sorbed dilemma about how an influx of people of a "different culture"
might change nations within Europe.

Which raises another question: just how insecure about a national sense of identity do you need to be to think that the arrival of
Muslim migrants might torpedo it? And how skewed are our priorities
if the overriding response to the devastating sight of thousands of desperate, drowning refugees is to wonder what they might do to our

"culture", or "traditions", or "values", or whatever proxy term for intolerance it is that you're using? Of course it's true that Europe is caught in a grim financial crisis, deepened by cruel austerity cuts, leading to an undignified scrabble for resources in the fifth-wealthiest country in the world. But there is much to learn from some of the popular responses to the refugee crisis - which is in stark contrast to official Europe's blameshifting and border-closing. Driven by a sense of care and empathy, the practical humanitarian assistance from groups and individuals across the continent should put European politicians to shame.

These are the people thinking about logistics: they are raising funds and taking supplies from Britain to the refugee camps in Calais and beyond. They are welcoming and helping refugees arriving on Greek islands after horrific journeys by sea.

They are outpacing assistance from governments and aid groups; one woman, from Cork, at the Jules Ferry camp near the Eurotunnel in France, describes how she became involved: "Our government has been weak in this respect... Suddenly we're like, 'Oh God, we can do it ourselves'." These volunteers on the ground have seen when things really aren't complicated - and have reacted with clarity and compassion and open hearts.

If there's one thing to wish for in 2016, it's that we understand and are honest about when a problem is complex and when it is not. And that an open, humane and straightforward response to the refugee crisis becomes the default, not a remarkable exception.

Rachel Shabi

January 2016

2016 COULD BE HORRENDOUS

Refugee crisis in the European Union

3 January 2016

FAILURE OF INTERNATIONAL GOVERNANCE

It was one of the defining images of 2015: an apparently endless column of people trudging wearily along roads in southern Europe, clutching plastic bags and suitcases. Syria is emptying out, on a scale that invokes images of Biblical migrations, and there seems to be no end to the exodus.

Like most people in Western Europe, I feel aghast and helpless in the face of human suffering on this scale. I wasn't alive during the Second World War but the parallels with the involuntary movement of people caused by the Nazis are as obvious as they are uncomfortable. In the late 1930s, the US and much of Europe closed its doors to hundreds of thousands of desperate would-be migrants who were trying to flee Hitler, refusing their requests for visas and condemning many to die in concentration camps.

No one should forget that Anne Frank and her family went into hiding in 1942 because they were what would now be called "failed asylum-seekers". There was nothing inevitable about the death of Anne, who might be alive today if the world's democracies had shown more compassion towards German Jews. Three-quarters of a century later, Western governments are still failing to provide safe, legal avenues of escape for people who face murder, arrest and torture at the hands of their own governments.

In the case of Syria, there is an additional threat from the religious fanatics of Islamic State (IS) and groups sympathetic to al-Qaeda. But the root cause of this latest refugee crisis is once again a fascist government that is prepared to commit atrocities to stay in power. Bashar al-Assad's Baath party was founded immediately after the Second World War by admirers of Hitler and Mussolini, and one of the main torture instruments in his prisons is known as the "German chair". The heart-rending columns of Syrian refugees are proof of a failure to act on promises made by the international community when pictures from the Nazi death camps emerged for the first time. There is no agreement, let alone anything approaching a big idea, about how to achieve what the vast majority of Syrians actually want: the possibility of returning to their country and resuming their lives in safety. It's a failure of international governance (not a phrase you hear very often these days) on a grand scale.

So, where are the institutions which were supposed to prevent such horrors happening again? Where, to be more precise, is the UN? The scale of the international community's failure to respond effectively to humanitarian crises was underlined last week by the outgoing UN High Commissioner for Refugees, Antonio Guterres. The Portuguese politician held the job for 10 years and pointed out that the number of displaced people had increased from 36 million to a

staggering 60 million in that period. Guterres blamed this development on the international community losing much of its capacity to
avoid or solve a "dramatic multiplication of conflicts" in the world.
That's the UN's job. But affluent countries are squabbling about who
will take Syrian refugees - David Cameron has offered to take a paltry
20,000 over five years - while children continue to drown in boats that
aren't even seaworthy. The Prime Minister's interest in foreign affairs
is too inconsistent to deserve being called a policy; he got rid of Colonel Gaddafi in Libya but sells arms to the monstrous Saudi
government, which is killing civilians in Yemen and executed almost
50 of its own citizens on yesterday. Last month, RAF planes joined the
US Air Force in bombing IS's military forces and economic interests in
Syria, while Russia appears to be using air strikes against the jihadists
as cover to target Assad's opponents.

I doubt whether many people are even aware that the UK held
the rotating presidency of the UN's most powerful body, the Security
Council, in November last year. Cameron certainly didn't seize the opportunity to come up with new ideas to break the stalemate created
by Russia's support for Assad. If that really is as great an obstacle as
some commentators suggest - and even Vladimir Putin might be getting fed up with his onerous protégé by now - it means that the UN is
simply not able to fulfil its primary role of maintaining international
peace and security.

It seems unlikely that the conflict in Syria can be brought to an
end without ground troops, and a UN force taking temporary control
of the country under a Security Council mandate seems the best solution. The idea has been welcomed by some British MPs but why isn't
Cameron, François Hollande or Barack Obama pushing for it? If the
UN's structure means that a single country can prevent it from protecting civilians and intervening in conflicts as savage as Syria's, then
the case for reform is unanswerable.

At the very least, the UN needs a permanent military force, ready
to be deployed at short notice, instead of having to respond to crises
on an ad hoc basis. In November last year, the latest month for which
figures are available, its entire peacekeeping force, drawn from its
member countries, amounted to little more than 106,000 police and
military personnel. They have to carry out all the UN's current peacekeeping missions, and many more would be needed to deal with the
different factions in Syria.

History shows that dictators are a perennial problem, causing huge suffering at home and creating refugee crises abroad. But the Syrian disaster confirms that even the leaders of democratic states, with a public commitment to universal human rights, are struggling to rise above narrow national interests. Instead of making the UN work, they're repeating the mistakes that caused so many needless deaths in the 20th century.

Joan Smith

4 January 2016

TESTING GERMANY'S TOLERANCE

The suspected arson attack on Germany's "model" migrant town could hardly have struck a more politically sensitive target.

Schwäbisch Gmünd, a community of 60,000 people in the state of Baden-Württemberg, is regarded as living proof of Chancellor Angela Merkel's claim that Germans "can manage" Europe's biggest refugee crisis since the Second World War. But, on Christmas Eve, suspected far-right supporters set fire to a brand new, and as yet empty, architect-designed asylum hostel for 120 people in the town's suburbs. Although no one was hurt, the attack rendered the building uninhabitable.

Hopes that refugees could move into the complex in early 2016 were crushed.

The incident was just one of more than 220 such suspected far-right attacks in 2015. But in Schwäbisch Gmünd it destroyed the notion that assimilation policies could somehow shield the town from violence. "It was incomprehensible - we have invested so much in integrating refugees and the policy is widely accepted," said Klaus Pavel, a leading regional member of Ms Merkel's conservatives.

More than 800 concerned citizens gathered around the Christmas tree on the town's cobbled 18th-century main square to condemn the attack. Describing the incident as "cowardly" Schwäbisch Gmünd's conservative mayor Richard Arnold proclaimed that his town was a "beacon of openness" which remained "opposed to stupidity and darkness".

Mr Arnold has staked his reputation on his town's handling of the refugee crisis.

Since Chancellor Merkel introduced her controversial "open-door refugee" policy late in the summer of 2015, many German towns have seen an influx of refugees and migrants - with more than one million people, mainly from the war-torn Middle East, Afghanistan and sub-Saharan Africa, having arrived in the country. Most live in requisitioned sports halls, disused aircraft hangars, empty barracks or heated tents.

Not so in Schwäbisch Gmünd. Half of the town's 800 refugees live in private households. Mr Arnold's 80-year-old parents, who live in a shared community flat, have taken in two refugees from Africa. One is Nigerian the other is from Gambia. "They have brought a breath of fresh air into the place," Mr Arnold insists. "Integration does not work if refugees live five to a room in a hostel, they have to get into private homes."

Mr Arnold's approach is known throughout Germany as the "Gmünder Weg" (the Gmünder Way). It aims to integrate refugees quickly by housing them in private accommodation or specially designed community flats. So far, 90 private flats and houses have been put at refugees' disposal. Schwäbisch Gmünd's tolerance may stem from the fact that its population grew by 30 per cent after 1945 thanks to the arrival of German refugees from Soviet-occupied eastern Europe.

All of today's refugees and migrants are offered German language courses from the outset. Most of the teachers are voluntary workers. The new arrivals are encouraged to join community associations such as choirs, clubs and even to support the fire brigade.

Near the end of last month, Ramin, a 20-year-old refugee from Afghanistan, had been accepted for a job as a rescue worker; his friend, Rodriguez, from Cameroon, had been voted on to a church council.

"Those who join in, get involved, get school qualifications and an apprenticeship should be allowed to stay," insists MrArnold. He believes that most refugees will be inclined to stay in Germany and the sooner they integrate, the better their prospects.

Yet not everything in Schwäbisch Gmünd reflects the town's "model refugee" image. Recently, Bright, a 20-year-old refugee from Nigeria and his friend Ken were busy dragging a decaying bed and a decrepit armchair into their asylum hostel in a disused former US

army barracks in the town's outlying Hardt district. Inside, the building was filthy, the walls scrawled with graffiti, the kitchen covered in
pools of water.

"The conditions here are disgusting," said Bright, who had fled
religious persecution and crossed the Mediterranean by boat to get to
Europe. "When people in here take off their clothes to wash, you can
see their bodies covered in rashes. We think it is because of the conditions here," he told The Independent.

One of Bright's hostel neighbours was a 37-yearold woman called
Mercy. Also from Nigeria, the single mother said she had spent the
past two years living and sleeping in one room in the former barracks
with her three children. The eldest, a boy, was 10. "He has problems
at school," she said. "The people here don't like blacks."

Mercy said she was hoping that after two years' wait she would
eventually be granted asylum in Germany. She said she was attending
German lessons and once joined in a city scheme for refugees to help
landscape municipal gardens. "We got no money. I did it to make them
happy. But blacks are not welcome here," she insisted. It seemed that
Bright, Ken and Mercy had not yet stepped on to the Gmünder Weg's
fast track to integration and success.

A 1950s housing estate separated their barrack hostel from the
fire-damaged new asylum home that fell victim to the Christmas Eve
attack. Outside one of the flats, a young German couple were unload-
ing their post-festivity shopping from their VW.

"There are plenty of people around here who have problems with
refugees," they admitted, without giving their names. "We've got
nothing against them personally but we don't much like the idea of a
new hostel parked right in front of our noses. They'll be sending their
kids to the local school next."

Mayor Richard Arnold is an ardent supporter of Angela Merkel.
But he is the first to admit that if the flow of refugees entering Germany continues at its present rate, his model migrant town will no
longer be able to cope. The prospect, he says, makes his "stomach
ache".

Tony Paterson

5 January 2016

THE END OF SCHENGEN?

Europe's passport-free Schengen zone is facing the biggest test of its 20-year existence after Sweden re-imposed controls on visitors crossing from Denmark across what was one of most open borders in the world.

Hours after the measures came into effect yesterday, Denmark announced it would slap new controls on its own border with Germany, while Berlin warned that the 26-nation zone of passport-free travel was now "in danger".

Six Schengen countries - Austria, Germany, France, Sweden, Denmark and non-EU member Norway - have reintroduced border checks as Europe struggles to cope with an unprecedented influx of refugees and migrants from conflict zones including Syria and Afghanistan.

The Danish Prime Minister, Lars Lokke Rasmussen, blamed Sweden for his own country's introduction of random border checks. "We are simply reacting to a decision made in Sweden. This is not a happy moment at all," he said. Without action, he added, the checks in Sweden could "increase the risk of a large number of illegal immigrants accumulating in and around Copenhagen".

Sweden's new identity controls target travellers crossing by train or bus from Denmark over the five-mile Öresund Bridge, or using ferry services. About 17,000 commuters a day cross the Öresund between the Danish capital, Copenhagen, and Malmo in Sweden. The rules, enforcing an ID check for travellers between the two nations for the first time in 50 years, meant that rail passengers had to exit their trains and show photo ID at checkpoints in Copenhagen before re-boarding to cross the bridge. Direct journeys from Copenhagen's main station to Sweden were cancelled, with the changes doubling the usual 40-minute commute time.

Denmark's rail company, DSB, along with ferry and bus companies, conducted the checks. Sweden's state-owned train operator, SJ, said last month that it would suspend services to and from Denmark if such a measure were introduced, as it would not have time to conduct the checks. The Danish Transport Minister, Hans Christian Schmidt, described the new measures as "extremely annoying" and suggested Sweden should pay for the checks, which DSB estimates will cost around £100,000 a day.

Sweden's new controls represent a turnaround for a nation which has taken in more asylum-seekers per capita than any other European country.

Although the left-leaning government initially welcomed the Syrian, Iraqi and Afghan refugees who swept across Europe last summer, it only expected about 100,000 to make it to Sweden, many of them through Denmark. The final figure was more than 160,000 and strained essential services.

Such scenes have been replicated across the continent, with more than one million refugees and migrants having arrived in Europe during 2015, and nations such as Hungary and Slovenia reinforcing the exterior borders of the Schengen zone.

The new controls are not just a reverse of the 1995 Schengen accord but also a setback to the post-1945 Nordic Council tradition of open borders that includes the five-nation Nordic Passport Union, which came into force in 1957. It was "a dark day for our Nordic region", said a former Swedish foreign minister, Carl Bildt. The German Chancellor, Angela Merkel, responded by calling for a "joint European solution" on the issue of refugees and migrants. Her spokesman, Steffen Seibert, said: "The solution won't take place on national borders between country A and country B."

A German foreign ministry spokesman, Martin Schaefer, added: "Schengen is very important but it is in danger."

However, Germany itself imposed controls at its Austrian border last September, just days after offering refuge to all Syrian nationals. Under Schengen rules, members can ask for a six-month exemption from the agreement on free circulation in exceptional circumstances.

Norway said last week that it would tighten its rules and turn back asylum-seekers without visas. Its right-leaning government said the draft law would create one of Europe's toughest immigration systems, making it more difficult to claim welfare benefits, and only allowing family reunifications after four years of work or education in Norway. About 30,000 people sought asylum in Norway last year, most crossing the border from Sweden.

The UN's special representative for migration, Peter Sutherland, said Europe should improve its external border controls and speed up asylum processing rather than retreating from Schengen. "Recreating borders across the EU will not answer anything, least of all, the humanitarian crisis we face," he said.

Elizabeth Collett, director of Migration Policy Institute Europe, said the new measures would do little to stop refugees.

"The political message to neighbours is, 'It's your turn, you deal with it.' But that just passes the problem along," she added. "None of the drivers that have led people to migrate have changed, given the conflict in Syria and instability elsewhere."

Leo Cendrowicz

11 January 2016

SETBACK FOR MIGRANTS AND WOMEN

It was a good week for implacable antiimmigration warriors, for extremists and regular right-wingers. Gleefully they turned up in newspapers and on radio and TV to denounce multiculturalism and Islam and declare that they were right all along. Non-Europeans were a threat to civilisation and a blight. Their message must have been welcomed by nationalists all across Europe. And who can really blame them? Women out celebrating New Year's Eve in Cologne and other German cities were stalked, surrounded, sexually assaulted, abused, humiliated and robbed by gangs of men, hundreds of them. Such incidents were also reported in Finland, Sweden and Switzerland. The onslaughts and thefts seemed to be well co-ordinated. The police watched the drama of sexual violence as if they were at a theatre and did nothing; the German media seemed cowed. Angela Merkel, who did the right thing by admitting desperate Syrian refugees, is now caught in a maelstrom.

According to witness and victim statements, most of the brutes looked Arab or African. Some, it turns out, were asylum seekers. Among the suspects are Algerians, Moroccans, Syrians, Iranians, an Iraqi, a Serbian, an American and a German.

Those of us on the left who believe in equality and justice for all have found these events intolerably hard to deal with. They have led to moral chaos and loss of faith. We need to get over the shock and find our voices. We must take on those who blame migrants and refugees for all vices and political failures. But more importantly, we must unconditionally damn the villains and defend the victims. Anti-racism is weak and unworthy unless it embraces the principles of feminism. Too often it doesn't.

How frightened and disgusted those women and girls must have been. The men who violated their bodies and integrity deserve no understanding, no mercy. Feminists are rightly outraged. I am outraged. These sex-crazed men obviously believe that a woman out in a public space is asking for it. Some come from cultures where sexism is embedded in families, communities and institutions. In Tahrir Square during the Arab Spring females were sexually assaulted and some raped. In India, women cannot safely go out on to the streets after dusk. Rape is endemic, almost normalised, in South Africa. Some minorities in Europe live by those same depraved values which, I agree, are uncivilised and deplorable.

The furious sexism that now engulfs Merkel and Henriette Reker, the mayor of Cologne, is as uncivilised and deplorable. These two remarkable women are under siege because they are seen as soft on refugees. Last October, Reker was stabbed in the throat by a man who detested her pro-refugee policies. After newspapers reported the Cologne attacks, a Facebook comment (by a woman) went viral: "I would puke when I read this and there are still so many deluded idiots who say 'welcome refugees'. Close the border now, for God's sake. Merkel belongs on the scaffold." Why is it acceptable to insult these female leaders? And to blame all refugees? "These monstrous men represent the tiniest fraction of the 1.1 million refugees who entered Germany last year. The overwhelming majority are law-abiding, and grateful to their host country." These words appeared in an editorial in a rightwing newspaper, which then went on to warn readers about the many unskilled young men coming into Europe from war zones and failed states. So, according to this leader writer, that black cleaner in your office, the Arab-looking dustman, the brown-skinned barista, is highly likely to assault your daughters, wives and sisters. You have been warned.

Was there no rape and molestation in Germany or elsewhere in Europe before these outsiders came in? Or are such crimes more heinous if committed by foreigners? A reader assaulted by fellow students at a prestigious university wrote to me last week: "The hypocrisy is disgusting. White men from public school fondled, groped and hand-raped me at an after-exam party. I had to leave halfway through my studies. I told my tutor and he told me to keep quiet for my own sake. Two years later I am at another uni and still frightened.

What happened in Cologne happens here too, on our streets at weekends and on campuses."

Rape statistics in all Western countries are shockingly high. The culture has changed, but behaviour has not. According to Rape Crisis, around 85,000 women and 12,000 men are raped each year in England and Wales. Half a million adults are also sexually assaulted. Child rape and molestation is also widespread. Though more crimes are reported and taken to court, conviction rates are still too low.

Admittedly, too many males from the South and East believe white women are easy and available. The British Pakistani grooming gangs acted on these prejudices. The Cologne thugs must have believed they were helping themselves to a sexual buffet freely proffered. However, the racial factor has been over-emphasised. Women of colour as well as white women were assaulted, including asylum-seekers, some of whom have bravely spoken to the media. The men betrayed generous Germany as well as other destitute, distressed asylum seekers who have now lost public sympathy. Joy will have spread among Isis recruits, fascists, purists and other enemies of diversity.

The culture clash today is not between natives and foreigners, the West and the rest, Islam and Judeo-Christianity, but between barbarians of all races and faiths and progressive people of all races and faiths who believe in human dignity, rights and equality. The left needs to wake up to these new schisms otherwise it will languish and rot on the wrong side of history.

Yasmin Alibhai-Brown

15 January 2016

NORWAY REFUSES ASYLUM TO REFUGEES

Norway is preparing to send over 5,500 refugees who crossed into the country from Russia on bicycles last year back across the border by the same mode of transport.

Police districts across Norway have been ordered to gather up and repair bikes that were abandoned by incoming refugees near the Storskog border crossing last year, after Norwegian authorities refused to grant asylum to the refugees who entered from Russia.

"We asked that the bikes which were left behind or claimed by the police to be gathered up for use by the foreigners who will be returned to Russia," Jan Erik Thomassen, a section head from Norway's National Police Directorate, said. "I can understand that it feels a bit awkward and odd."

Despite the Arctic conditions this time of year, a border agreement between Russia and Norway means that bicycles have become the only way for refugees to cross from one country to the other. The agreement bars people from crossing over the border on foot and bans drivers from ferrying people into the country in their cars without documents.

Norwegian authorities said they hope Russia will allow the refugees to re-enter its Russian territory by bus, which would reduce costs and provide safer passage for those making the journey. But Russia, which has remained hostile to refugees despite the influx of migrants into Europe last year, seems unlikely to comply.

Most of the refugees who travelled to Storskog through Russia's Arctic city of Murmansk hail from Syria. Braving sub-zero temperatures in the hopes of receiving asylum in Norway, refugees say that travelling through Russia is a cheaper alternative than other means of getting to Europe.

"To be honest, it costs much less than going to Turkey and from Turkey getting on a small, small, boat to cross to Greece, and then from Greece to Europe itself," one Syrian refugee crossing the border from Murmansk into Norway told ABC last November.

The situation was exacerbated further in November last year, when Norway announced that it would immediately expel asylum-seekers who had originated from Russia. Moscow answered with a tit-for-tat measure, and both countries have since sent refugees back and forth.

Despite over a 60 per cent rise in the number of applicants for asylum last year - including around 12,000 Syrians - Russia's Federal Migration Service awarded refugee status to less than 9 per cent of the total applicants.

More than a million people landed on Europe's shores last year, with most travelling through Turkey and disembarking on Greek islands just a short - but dangerous - hop across the Aegean Sea, which can cost refugees thousands of pounds, compared with the hundreds that refugees reportedly pay for bikes to take the route across Russia.

The EU's top migration official warned that efforts to manage the refugee crisis are failing as more countries tighten border security.

Nadia Beard

16 January 2016
EUROPE MUST BRACE ITSELF FOR A 2016 ONSLAUGHT

One million more refugees and migrants will try to enter Europe through the Eastern Mediterranean and Balkans in 2016, according to new UN projections.

The report, from the UNHCR, also predicts increasing numbers of women and children.

More than a million crossed into Europe in 2015 in one of the largest movements of people since the Second World War, and with continuing conflict in Syria and Iraq, discrimination against minorities in Afghanistan, and conflict and poverty in north and east Africa, the report says Europe should expect no slowdown.

In recent months, an increasing percentage of refugees and migrants have been women and children, it adds. "This trend may continue to rise as more families are travelling," it states. "In addition an increasing number of reports suggest that women and children are being sent ahead or trying to join their male relatives who already in destination countries."

The international community was caught "unprepared" by the crisis in 2015, and will require a more coordinated response in 2016 to address the humanitarian and security needs of refugees and migrants, the report adds.

Arrivals to Europe via the perilous Mediterranean Sea crossing rose over the course of the year before peaking in October, according to the UNCHR's analysis. Of those arriving via the Eastern Mediterranean and Balkan routes, 55 per cent are men, 17 per cent women and 28 per cent children. Syrians, Afghans and Iraqis make up the largest national groups of migrants and refugees.

Charlie Cooper

17 January 2016

TRAFFICKING NOW RIVALS THE TRADE IN ILLICIT DRUGS

Human smugglers made a record profit last year of between $3bn and $6bn (£2bn-£4bn) by exploiting the misery of refugees - which means governments must up their game or risk further growth of this ruthless industry, the head of Europol has told The Independent on Sunday.

The business of human smuggling is now in the "Champions League" of criminal enterprises in Europe, Rob Wainwright said, close to rivalling the trade in illicit drugs. New research by the EU's law enforcement body based on debriefings with 1,500 asylum-seekers, refugees and economic migrants showed that 90 per cent had paid a criminal gang to reach Europe.

With the UNHCR estimating that more than a million people have fled war, poverty and persecution in the past year risking their lives on the clandestine journey to Europe, that "means a lot of people making a lot of money", Mr Wainwright said.

"We also know that, on average, each migrant is paying between $3,000 and $6,000 to a criminal facilitator for their journey. So you do the simple math, and you're up to a turnover in 2015 of between $3bn-$6bn. They are big figures. It's running into billions of dollars made by criminal networks in one year alone in Europe."

"Last year has been seismic in the development of the people-smuggling trade in Europe in particular, and we are now talking about its being a multibillion-dollar industry in the way it hasn't before, and the Champion's League of criminal sectors in Europe alongside drugs."

The criminal networks stretch from sub-Saharan Africa to Scandinavia, with tens of thousands of people involved in the trade. Mr Wainwright said that Europol identified 10,700 suspects last year alone, hinting at the scale of the illicit enterprise. The facilitators range from petty criminals, making fake passports, to taxi drivers taking migrants across countries and over borders, to established organised crime syndicates.

A person fleeing their home will pay different smuggling gangs at different points throughout their journey. A Syrian may have to pay to leave their country without detection by the security forces, then buy fake documents in Turkey, before purchasing their perilous passage on a rubber dingy or boat launched into the waves, towards Greece.

If they arrive safely on Europe's shores, another smuggler is engaged to taken them over the buffer of Balkan states to reach the passportfree Schengen zone and the chance of a safe life in richer nations such as Germany, Austria or Sweden. With Hungary and a number of other countries in Europe shutting down their borders and building fences, the migrants are forced to part with ever-increasing amounts of money to reach safety.

Abuses are reported all along the migration routes: smugglers disappear with a family's life savings, scuttle boats on purpose to stop anyone returning to shore, or sell the most desperate people to kidnapping and extortion gangs.

With many of the people-smuggling networks now getting involved in other criminal enterprises such as narcotics trafficking, security services and governments need to redouble their efforts to shut them down, Mr Wainwright said.

"Criminals that were active in the drugs business or predominantly active in the people-smuggling business are now turning their hand to a bit of both and are finding that their contacts and networks and routes and methods of concealment can work in both fields."

The first challenge for governments and policing agencies was dealing with the scale of the new arrivals. If a million more people want to come to Europe this year, there is "a natural demand for these criminal services, which will therefore sustain a long-term growth model for this particular criminal sector", Mr Wainwright said.

"We're going to have to up our game in terms of dismantling this criminal infrastructure in a more successful way then we have done in the past," he added.

Countries in the EU needed to work on a coordinated response to the crisis, both at the entry point to the Union and in intelligence-sharing to target the criminal kingpins. Better planning of international arrest operations would help, he said, while police forces across the bloc needed to prioritise complaints related to smuggling.

And intelligence-sharing and cooperation between nations was all the more important, given indications that terror groups may be now exploiting the chaotic response to the refugee crisis.

Two members of the gang of ISaffiliated attackers who killed 130 people in Paris on 13 November had apparently entered Europe using the Balkan migration route, and Mr Wainwright said it was crucial to make sure Greece was supplied with the technology, manpower and resources to carry out effective security screening of all new arrivals.

"When you put the external border of the EU under such strain that it has to cope with a million new arrivals at just a few of the external border points, then you can see how difficult it is to run a systematic and reliable screening process," he said. "This is the single most important thing to get right: to make sure that we can help the Greek authorities, who have been swamped."

Charlotte McDonald-Gibson

23 January 2016

COULD THE REFUGEE CRISIS REALLY BREAK UP THE EU?

Yesterday's 43 new deaths by drowning in the Aegean Sea brought Europe's migration crisis sharply back into focus just as the French Prime Minister, Manuel Valls, warned that unless the flow of refugees is better managed, it could cause the break-up of the European Union.

How serious is the refugee crisis? More than a million migrants and refugees came to Europe last year, mostly via Turkey. Although winter was expected to slow the pace, 35,000 have arrived in the first three weeks of January, compared with 1,600 for the whole month last year.

How has the EU responded? There have been many initiatives since last spring, and EU leaders have discussed the issue at six separate summits, but most measures have been inadequate or slow, or both. They include relocation and resettlement efforts, a new border control police, and a deal with Turkey to stop refugees heading to Europe.

What went wrong with relocation? The plan to relocate 160,000 people more evenly across the EU was immediately controversial, as eastern countries like Hungary pointed out that refugees wanted to go to Berlin, not Budapest. The results are pitiful: only 331 have been relocated since September. The plans to resettle refugees from outside Europe have not been much better: only 779 of the 5,331 due in 2015 had been effectively resettled.

What is being done to police the EU's borders? Last month, EU leaders backed plans for a European Border and Coast Guard, aimed mainly at Greece and Italy, where most refugees have landed. It would ensure asylum-seekers are screened and registered before a decision is taken on whether they can stay. It will come too late for most leaders. Dutch Prime Minister Mark Rutte said: "We need to get a grip on this issue in the next six to eight weeks."

Can Turkey help? The EU signed a €3bn (£2.3bn) deal with Turkey aimed at stemming the flow. Turkey is hosting 2.2 million refugees from Syria, Iraq and other war zones. But EU finance ministers have yet to agree who should pay; EU officials complain Turkey is not playing its part and Ankara says the €3bn isn't enough.

Does migration hurt Europe? Economically, it is a boon: an IMF report on Wednesday said EU states that take in the most people will get the biggest windfall - worth an extra 1.1 per cent growth in Austria, Germany, and Sweden by 2020. Migrants may also fill the demographic shortfall from Europe's shrinking population. The EU's active labour force of 240 million would fall to 207 million by 2050, even if migration runs at the present level. If it halts, the workforce would shrink to 169 million.

Why did Germany open and then close its doors? The German Chancellor, Angela Merkel, earned worldwide praise for inviting Syrian refugees to come to her country. But a political backlash at home forced her to change tack, closing Germany's borders. The mood has further soured after New Year's Eve assaults on women in Cologne, blamed on Muslim migrants.

Will the crisis bring Europe's borders back? The passport-free Schengen zone across much of the EU is being severely tested. Six countries - Austria, Germany, France, Sweden, Denmark and non-EU member Norway - have reintroduced temporary border checks. The European Commission President Jean-Claude Juncker warns dismantling Schengen would cost £2.3bn a year in lost business. The European Council President Donald Tusk says unless the EU makes progress in the next two months, Schengen could fail.

What about Greece, the weak link in the refugee trail? Under EU rules, asylumseekers must register in the first safe country they reach. But this "Dublin" regulation put huge administrative burdens on Greece and Italy, and is widely ignored: most refugees arrive on deserted beaches and travel by land to countries like Germany and

Sweden. A rule change due in March may replace this with a quota system.

Would this mean more migrants come to Britain? It's unlikely to affect the relatively few asylum-seekers who enter the UK, which has no land border with Europe and retains border checks. Britain has an opt-out on asylum policy, so could choose not to apply it. Britain's share of asylum claims has fallen to 3.5 per cent last year. But it would mean renegotiating the associated rules under which Britain returns 1,000 migrants a year to the country where they first arrived.

Could this all affect Britain's renegotiation with the EU? David Cameron aims to cut the number of EU citizens travelling to Britain to work, not asylum-seekers. But the crisis plays into the hands of those seeking the UK's withdrawal.

Leo Cendrowicz

February 2016

NEARING SATURATION?

Port of Kos, Greece, 4 kilometers from the Turkish coast, 23 January 2016

8 February 2016

EXHAUSTED 'CAPACITY TO ABSORB'

Turkey warned yesterday that it has exhausted its "capacity to absorb" refugees amid mounting pressure to accept a wave of Syrians driven from their homes by a major Russian-backed offensive. Angela Merkel, the German Chancellor, was due to travel to Turkey today in an effort to gain Ankara's help in slowing the tide of refugees entering the European Union. On the eve of her visit, the Turkish Deputy Prime Minister, Numan Kurtulmus, said that his nation was now hosting three million refugees, 2.5 million of them Syrian.

He said that, though it had reached its limits, Turkey would ultimately take more people because "in the end, these people have nowhere else to go".

However, as darkness fell yesterday Turkey had yet to open its Bab al-Salam border crossing to northern Aleppo province, where the United Nations estimates that 35,000 people are "newly displaced". Though the UN said yesterday that only 2,500 to 3,000 people remained at the border crossing itself, tens of thousands more were said to have sought shelter in nearby towns and camps that were bursting at the seams even before the latest influx.

Dr Osama Abo el-Ezz, a Syrian doctor who travelled to Turkey from Aleppo on Saturday night via a different crossing, told The Independent he had encountered many families who had taken refuge in the rural, rebel-held areas to the west of the city.

"They are hungry, they are sleeping on the ground," he said. "They are waiting for some kind of help. Every day there are about 10 to 20 people killed in Aleppo city by the Russian planes and by bombing by the regime," he said. "The situation in Aleppo is getting worse and worse."

With the help of Russia, Iran and Hezbollah, the Syrian government has made a series of gains in Aleppo province. Last week, it severed the sole main rebel supply line from Turkey. Yesterday, heavy fighting was reported around the village of Ratyan as part of a campaign to slice rebel-held territory in two.

Those living in the eastern part of Aleppo, an opposition stronghold since 2012, fear that they are on the verge of being totally encircled and placed under siege.

Dr Abo el-Ezz warned of an impending crisis in the city. "The hospitals have been storing up some fuel and some medications - but not enough," he said.

"The people have no way to store anything because they are poor. Aid organisations have been storing food and water but I don't think it is enough for all the people in the city."

He said that there were already shortages of food, medicine and clean water as well as near-constant bombardment.

Mr Kurtulmus estimated that "in the worst-case scenario" as many as one million more refugees could flee the Syrian city of Aleppo and surrounding areas. That would present a huge challenge both for Turkey and for Europe.

Ms Merkel's visit comes amid reports that 70,000 migrants have entered the EU from Turkey via Greece since the start of the year, despite a €3bn (£2.3bn) deal between Ankara and Brussels aimed at stemming the flow of people.

She is facing growing domestic pressure over her "open-door" policy that enabled more than one million refugees to enter the country in 2015. A recent German television poll showed that some 80 per cent of voters now think that her government has "lost control" of the situation.

During meetings with politicians and officials, she is expected to urge Turkey to police its maritime border with Greece more effectively and to halt migrant trafficking. But her visit is complicated by the latest wave of people displaced in northern Aleppo.

Laura Pitel and Dan Paterson

10 February 2016

'A QUICK, KIND-HEARTED RESPONSE'

It takes Ben Harrison a long time to walk around the refugee camp just outside Calais, he says, "because I get mobbed". This blond 20-year-old, who was born in Dulwich, organises housing here and is therefore highly in demand. People spot his yellow raincoat and race through the sandy wind and muddy puddles to ask him for help.

I find him chain-smoking roll-ups, surrounded by excited boys who all want his attention, and talking to a man from Pakistan who has nowhere to sleep. Harrison, who people here refer to as "well-spoken Ben" and who works 12-hour days, remains calm: "We will come to you, my friend," he says, stopping to ask one of the boys if he has been to the clinic to treat his chest infection.

"It's hard to predict how the day will go," he tells me as we walk past a "David Cameron Street" sign, an advert for Pilates class in the camp and graffiti reading "London Spirit".

Around 7,000 people have sought shelter in this small, dusty settlement off the motorway, some fleeing dangerous conditions. Alongside the tightly clustered makeshift homes where everyone is keen to offer guests sugary tea, refugees run impressively wellstocked corner shops, hairdressers, bike shops and a radio station where they make podcasts.

The French government won't recognise the camp, which means the UN is not officially allowed in and it is difficult for larger aid agencies to help. Instead, it has fallen to volunteers such as Harrison to fill the gaps and provide what playwright Joe Robertson, 25, calls "a quick, kind-hearted response, tailored to the people, for something that is happening on our doorstep".

That has taken many forms, from London's street-food chefs, who are here feeding people, to nail artist f Sharmadean Reid, who visited last month. She sorted donations in a warehouse and cheered up refugees with manicures. Robertson and his friend Joe Murphy run the Good Chance Theatre. It is crowdfunded, supported by director Stephen Daldry and was given its name because refugees always say: "There's a good chance I may get away tonight."

"Community structures keep people going," says Robertson. "These are things that refugees haven't had since they left their homes and it's inspiring to see what they are able to create. The theatre is apolitical and we don't ask people to tell their stories. It is one of the few places where people can do something that isn't about getting their next meal."

Robertson takes me on a tour past the restaurants which the refugees have set up, and we meet Marie, a fashion videographer who has moved here from Dalston and plans to set up a juice bar in the camp "so people can get fresh food and vitamins". She is handing out coconut cake with Viv Dale, who works as a chef at Ella Woodward's new café, Mae Deli, in Marylebone, and lives in Walthamstow. Dale says: "We try to offer a range of food because choice is the last dignifying luxury people have."

"The camp has changed since Robertson and Harrison arrived four months ago, when there were only three water supply points for thousands of people. Harrison says: "I thought I'd help with educational projects but there were already schools and there was a pressing need for housing. No nationality is favoured — in August, people would fight over things like shoes but now they see there is a system for getting to people based on need and they respect it because it is seen to be fair."

Harrison, whose father is a lawyer and mother was a pianist, is on a second gap year. He was working as a private tutor in Moscow, planning to take a job in an investment bank "but I saw this on the news and came. I got a bus from Calais by myself, with refugees. I tailed them at 100m because I was nervous."

"Since then he has put up more than 1,000 houses. He plans to study History and Economics at Yale in September but for now he wants to tell me about the Afghan refugees who were interpreters for the British army but aren't being given asylum, and the huge influx of unaccompanied children who are here. He keeps in touch with the refugees: "The story doesn't end if they make it to England. Some become depressed and try to come back here."

"There are more than 22 nationalities in the camp, and Harrison says "the volunteers add to that melting pot". They played football against the refugees recently but lost 3-1.

Tom Radcliffe, 49, a Zen priest who runs the charity Help Calais, tells me: "The average volunteer here is a white, middle-class English liberal person aged 20 to 35. They bring an enormous amount of energy, willingness to muck in and a lack of cynicism but many burn out dealing with suffering. To continue long-term we are looking at training people."

The camp is supplied by a warehouse that is a 10-minute drive away, near the Calais Wine Superstore where signs advertise "deals for the Franglais". They also try to send supplies to a camp in Dunkirk, where there are more women and children than in Calais, but the French government has made it harder to enter than the Jungle.

House music is playing and a group of teenagers are loading a van with boxes of ornamental cauliflowers from Abel & Cole. A 14-year-old boy tells me that he came with his mother, who works in fashion and is home schooling him in their trailer. He is glad she brought him. In the kitchen, Jo Case, 28, a musician from Stoke Newington, is preparing a delivery of scallops and outside Tom, 27, is trying on the ski wear that has been donated. It's warm, unlike the wedding dresses and heels that were sent over recently. He is from Tottenham and says: "I do a bit of hospitality work there but I'm more useful here. It's busy on weekends." A lawyer and a City worker from London were among last weekend's volunteers.

It's presided over by Hettie Colquhoun, 23, who works with L'Auberge des Migrants and Help Refugees. She runs a tight ship, yelling at people to wear their hi-vis vests in the warehouse and has only had one weekend off in four-and-a-half months, visiting a fellow volunteer who is doing a ski season in Morzine: "I didn't realise I needed time off until I didn't manage to get the train initially. It was hard to leave because people kept talking to me. I'll be here for as long as I can afford it. If I was at home I'd be burning a hole in my pocket in different way. We are doing a grand job but it needs to be recognised by the government as a humanitarian crisis." She hasn't been to university but is doing an Open University course in forensic psychology.

Back at the camp, Robertson is picking up tear gas canisters next to the London Calling graffiti that Banksy recently came and added to with a picture of Steve Jobs, the son of a Syrian migrant. He says "lots of people say that it looks like Glastonbury after 10 years here". There are kitchens run by people who usually use their equipment for yoga festivals, while Glastonbury and Leeds festivals have donated tents and boots.

Radcliffe says: "There was a community feel here, like a festival, but it is getting grim, with bad weather and there being no way out." There is a high suicide rate in the camp and a narcotics anonymous group has been set up because many of the refugees haven't drunk before and then become hooked on strong beer bought from French supermarkets.

Police recently cleared a huge area which Robertson says was problematic: "You aren't just moving tents, you are moving communities, people live with others from the same country." He tells me about an Iraqi man at the camp who was on a boat to Europe with his pregnant sister. The engine failed so he and six other men tied their belts to the boat and towed it to shore.

Across the way are the white shipping containers set up by the French government for people to live in. "They have heating," says Robertson. "But you need to register and give fingerprints so many are reticent to sign up."

Volunteer Liz Clegg, 50, has become a de facto mother to many of the boys who are here alone, tells me that they don't accept children in the containers because they say they can't protect them with all the men who are there.

Clegg and her daughter Inca, 23, work with Citizens UK to help the unaccompanied minors in the camp. She had her phone stolen this morning but there is "an army of kids who will help her get it back". She introduces me to a boy who tries to run away to Dunkirk every night because he heard it's easier to get to the UK from there, dodging criminal gangs, and another who is 13 and has relatives in the UK.

They are playing with a dirty electric thermometer they have found at the camp. "That boy has relatives in the UK and is under 16 so he technically he has a right to be there but he is stuck here," says Clegg.

Another boy runs up and shows Robertson some papers, pointing at the line saying he has an asylum interview in Calais next week. "Bambino, that's great," says Robertson, explaining: "Lots of boys don't want to claim in France because their experience so far has been negative. They're scared of French police brutality. Traffickers, who they came over with, told them not to engage with authorities until they reach the UK."

Inside the Good Chance dome, London group Pan Arts is running a mime workshop with refugees. "One day feels like a week here," says Kirsten, a volunteer. Robertson, who is planning a recce to Dunkirk to see if they can do anything there, says: "Boys come here all the time when there's nothing to do. They are losing their minds. We couldn't leave now because it is a lifeline. We will stay for as long as it is safe and we are allowed to be here."

As we leave, we pass Ellis Cresswell, 27, a data analyst from Hackney who is up a ladder fixing a tarpaulin roof. "I took a week off work and came," she says. "Politicians can mess things up and doing something felt right. This could easily be us and we'd be upset if no one helped."

Susannah Butter

19 February 2016

SLOWING THE FLOW OF REFUGEES

German Chancellor Angela Merkel last night pushed EU leaders to keep faith in a €3bn (£2.3bn) deal with Turkey aimed at slowing the flow of refugees to Europe, as Austria insisted that it would push ahead with a cap on the number of people it takes in.

The refugee plans with Turkey, drawn up at the end of last year, would see Ankara tightening controls to prevent the two million Syrians currently in Turkish refugee camps from heading to Europe.

Only parts of the plan have been applied, and its effects have been hard to discern: the number of refugees having crossed the sea in the first six weeks of 2016 has significantly increased compared to the same period last year.

Frustrations over an inability to put a plan into effect has led to a number of EU nations beginning to tighten border controls, and Austria's Chancellor Werner Faymann said yesterday that his country would push ahead with plans - announced this week - to let in no more than 3,200 people and cap asylum claims at 80 per day.

"It is unthinkable forAustria to take on the asylum seekers for the whole of Europe," Mr Faymann said on arriving at a two-day EU leaders' summit in Brussels aimed at helping to end Europe's fragmented response to the crisis.

The plan drew a strong rebuke from the EU's top migration official, Dimitris Avramopoulos, who told Austria yesterday that a cap on the number of people who can apply for asylum is unlawful.

In a letter to Austrian interior minister Johanna Mikl-Leitner, Mr Avramopoulos wrote: "Austria has a legal obligation to accept any asylum application that is made on its territory or at its border."

He added that a ceiling on asylum-seekers "would be plainly incompatible with Austria's obligations" under EU and international law.

In response, Mr Faymann said yesterday that "Legal opinions will be answered by lawyers. Politically I say: we'll stick to it".

Ms Merkel insisted that a deal was the key to resolving the EU's migration crisis.

"We want to give priority to the implementation of the EU-Turkey migration agenda, including the protection of our external borders," she said when she arrived at the summit. "It is good if EU and Turkey share the burden, but we need protection of external borders, we have to find ways to allow legal migration."

Mrs Merkel said that if Turkey succeeds in holding back refugees, it would give EU breathing space to set up registration systems and border guards along Greece's long, unprotected coastline, where most of the refugees have been arriving.

But she is facing tough resistance from some of the EU's eastern members, who say the EU needs to seal Greece's borders to Macedonia and Bulgaria in April if the Turkey deal fails. EU officials also fear that Austria's restrictions will be copied by the countries on the main Balkan passage into northern Europe: Slovenia, Croatia, Serbia and Macedonia have said they will also set up new roadblocks along the way.

Although Ms Merkel says more time is needed for the measures agreed with Turkey to take effect, many officials suspect Ankara of dragging its feet in the hopes of securing more EU funding.

"The numbers are still too high at this stage, which will have to be improved," said Dutch Prime Minister Mark Rutte.

Mrs Merkel last week met Turkish Prime Minister Ahmet Davutoglu in Ankara and said the only way to end the flood of illegal immigrants was to allow the EU to screen refugees on Turkish soil and bring in legally those who qualify for asylum.

More than 76,000 refugees have made the sea crossing from Turkey to the Greek islands so far this year, up from less than 5,000 in the same period in 2015, according to the United Nations' refugee agency.

Leo Cendrowicz

20 February 2016

WELCOME TO EUROPE?

It was an aluminium factory. Then it became a municipal recycling centre. Now, the echoing warehouse on the Greek island of Chios is processing people.

Opened last weekend after a huge rush to be ready in time for an EU summit on Thursday, the hilltop facility is one of five "hotspots" set up on the islands at the behest of Brussels. By registering and fingerprinting the arrivals, authorities hope to impose some order after the chaotic scenes of last summer, when a million people arrived in Europe by sea alone - 800,000 of them from Greece via Turkey. But the idea remains dogged by both practical problems and huge unanswered questions about what happens next.

The setting for the Chios "hotspot" is beautiful - a drive up from the coast twists past lemon and orange trees and verges dotted with anemones. The centre is less charming: a concrete hulk surrounded by tall wire fencing.

Beyond the gates is a giant, dusty warehouse that reverberates to the sound of chatter in Arabic, Kurdish and Farsi. Having arrived on dinghies hours earlier, hundreds of weary parents from Syria, Iraq, Afghanistan and Iran cluster together on chairs while their children make mischief at their feet. The elderly recline on wooden pallets with blankets pulled up around their necks. Everyone says that they want to go to Germany.

Organised into numbered groups, everyone waits their turn to file along steel barriers and into cabins where police officers from across Europe verify their identity and put them into a database. It is part of a drive by EU leaders to tighten security, after it emerged the ringleader of the Paris attacks passed through the island of Leros.

Such was the hurry to get this place ready that workmen are still drilling inside and outside the hangar. There are no staff to clean and on the first day, there was not enough water for the toilets. EU border staff say that their computers are not yet properly hooked up to the databases they need.

Despite these glitches, the Chios hotspot - along with one that opened in Lesbos in October - is the one faring best out of four centres declared "ready to function" by the Greek Defence Minister on Tuesday.

In Samos, aid workers say there is no electricity and staff have been working in the dark. On Kos, everything has been held up by protests from locals who are worried and angry about the impact on tourism. On the first day in Leros, 600 people arrived and were promptly sent to an old camp because there were no staff to run the new hotspot.

European officials asked Greece to build hotspots last autumn, but for months nothing happened. Amid threats that Greece could be kicked out of the Schengen open border zone, on 31 January came a sudden scramble. With just two weeks to get the job done, the Greek government called in the army. In Chios the task fell to Lt-Col Lolos Charalambos, who would clearly rather be almost anywhere other than here.

"It's much easier for me to be a commander in a camp with my soldiers," he says wistfully. But he believes that he completed his mission successfully and is pleased to see that the refugees and migrants are calm and relatively relaxed. "I look at their faces and I see they are OK - that's the satisfaction for us."

For all the fanfare, few believe that these facilities will solve the vast challenge of the biggest refugee crisis since the Second World War. For a start, there is the question of numbers. The capacity of the Chios hotspot is 1,000 people but on Thursday at least 1,400 people arrived. The island was forced to use the old town centre camps for overspill.

Despite initiatives to encourage people to stay in Turkey and crack down on smuggling routes, that influx is expected to increase further as the weather warms up and the seas calm down. Even bigger than the practical problems are the many unanswered questions about the role these centres will play in controlling the flow of people towards the rest of Europe.

Many expect that the border with Macedonia - already closed to all but Syrians, Afghans and Iraqis - will soon completely shut. Joe Kuper, a Londoner running the UN refugee agency's response in Chios, warns that a backlog could quickly build up in a country still facing the fallout from the catastrophic 2009 debt crisis. "This is why it is important that the Greek authorities are prepared and have in place a contingency plan to receive and support refugees," he says.

Whether people stay put or seek alternative, riskier routes depends partly on their view of the likelihood of making it to Europe in a more regulated fashion. EU states have promised to relocate 160,000 asylum-seekers from Greece and Italy. So far, just 497 people have been taken.

There also needs to be a way to turn back those deemed ineligible to enter the EU. Last year, only 33,590 people were returned either voluntarily or by force. In December, a group of 31 Pakistanis was dispatched to Islamabad, only to be sent straight back after their government said that they had been illegally deported.

Alexis Tsipras, the Greek Prime Minister, has pleaded for help on returns to stop Greece becoming a "warehouse for human souls". Yesterday, Mr Tsipras met with Angela Merkel and François Hollande amid growing concern about Greece's "lack of control" over thousands of migrants crossing its borders. Officials said leaders at the talks argued over conflicting national reactions to the migrant influx, and the potential collapse of Europe's border-free travel.

The European Commission has given Greece three months to restore order on its borders, but few believe Athens will be able to meet the deadline. At present, the Chios hotspot is not acting as a detention centre - after being registered, the newcomers are given a temporary

visa and allowed to buy ferry tickets to the mainland. But, given the
wire fences and the hardening mood in Europe, some believe that
could soon be the purpose of the hotspots.

Laura Pitel

25 February 2016

'WAREHOUSE OF HUMAN SOULS'

Europe's ministers were today locked in wrangling over the migrant crisis after Greece warned it cannot become a "warehouse of
human souls".

EU interior ministers meeting in Brussels were expected to hear
plans drawn up by Austria and eight Balkan countries wanting to restrict the numbers entering their borders.

More than 100,000 migrants have reached Europe this year, most
via the Balkans. With numbers expected to soar in the warmer months
ahead, officials are warning the crisis could threaten the existence of
the European Union.

The countries have pledged to accept only those they deem to be
in need of protection, which has been interpreted by some as only Syrians and Iraqis.

Macedonia enacted the measures at its border with Greece over
the weekend, leaving thousands of Afghans stranded in Greece.

After Austria imposed new border controls yesterday, interior
minister Johanna Mikl-Leitner said the measures were a "chain reaction of reason" and warned the crisis could threaten the EU's survival.

Today's meeting was given extra urgency after Greece's prime
minister said it would block future EU agreements if other member
states refused to share the burden of refugees.

"Greece will not agree to deals (in the EU) if a mandatory alloca-
tion of burdens and responsibilities among member countries is not
secured," warned Alexis Tsipras. He told MPs he "will not accept turning the country into a permanent warehouse of souls with Europe
continuing to function as if nothing is happening".

He said it was unacceptable for EU partners to dump the burden
of the crisis on Greece, forcing it to shoulder a weight disproportionate to its size.

"We did and will continue to do everything we can to provide warmth, essential help and security to uprooted, hounded people. We will either be in a union of common rules for all or everyone will do as they please: we will not accept the latter."

Holland's interior minister Klaas Dijkhoff backed Hungary's right to hold a referendum on migrant quotas.

Budapest wants to challenge the EU's decision to relocate 160,000 Syrian refugees across Europe, which was carried despite fierce opposition from Hungary, the Czech Republic, Romania and Slovakia. So far just 598 refugees have been relocated, a mere 0.4 per cent of the target. Hungary has taken none of its 1,294 quota.

John Dunne

March 2016

EUROPEAN UNION TURNS NASTY

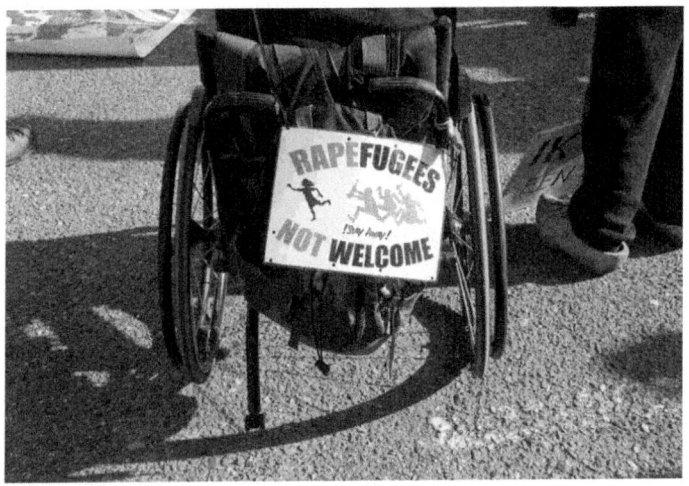

Protest against refugee camp, Enschede, Netherlands, 13 February 2016

4 March 2016

'DON'T COME TO EUROPE'

Economic migrants should not even contemplate coming illegally to Europe, the EU warned yesterday before a last-ditch attempt to stop the tide of people arriving on the continent's shores. Donald Tusk, President of the European Council, issued a strongly-worded warning to the those tempted to join the wave of refugees from Syria and Iraq in search of work.

Speaking in Athens before a key EU summit on Monday, he appealed to all potential illegal economic migrants: "Do not come to Europe. Do not risk your lives and your money. It is all for nothing.

Greece, or any other European country, will no longer be a transit country."

More than a million people arrived in Europe by sea last year and the flow is continuing. Balkan states and Austria have responded with strict border limits, creating a backlog in Greece and triggering a political crisis that may destroy the key EU principle of freedom of movement.

Mr Tusk was in Ankara for talks with Turkish leaders, who are seen as a vital part of solving the crisis. Turkey is home to 2.5 million Syrians and the starting point for most of those voyaging to Europe by boat. Mr Tusk wants Turkey to accept migrants turned away by Europe.

Laura Pitel

5 March 2016

REFUGEE CHILDREN SEXUALLY ABUSED IN THE 'JUNGLE'

Teenage boys are being raped in the Calais Jungle, aid workers have claimed, amid concerns over the lack of child protection measures in place in the refugee camp - and the risks of abuse facing thousands of displaced children across the continent.

Medical volunteers helping those camped outside the French town told The Independent they have treated seven boys aged between 14 and 16 in the past six months who claimed to have been raped. They all had injuries consistent with these claims.

In four cases, the boys required surgery. Only one attended hospital, however, with the others refusing treatment for fear of repercussions or through shame at having been abused.

The Independent has spoken to a GMC-registered doctor to whom the volunteers reported the incidents. He confirmed knowledge of the cases. He said he was aware of six or seven cases involving the rape of minors, including one gang rape of a 13-year-old Sudanese boy. He added that he had reported cases to an international child protection agency but to his knowledge no action had been taken.

Europol, the EU's law enforcement agency, has also raised concerns that unaccompanied refugee children across the continent are at high risk of sexual exploitation.

In January, a senior representative of Europol estimated that 10,000 unaccompanied children had gone missing within Europe.

Volunteers in the Calais camp have spoken out about the lack of procedure in reporting serious cases of sexual abuse. They add that the French government's refusal to classify the camp as a humanitarian crisis is causing major child protection issues.

"If I took one of the boys to the police and said 'I'm one of the medics and I know this boy has been sexually abused', I could guarantee they would shrug their shoulders and continue their conversation," said one of the volunteers.

"I have three boys of my own and this is horrendous," they added. "These boys would have left their homes and their parents would have thought they were safe and that they were going to a better life, fleeing violence and they end up at 14 being raped in a refugee camp. That it is going on in Europe makes it even more unacceptable."

The volunteers said they referred the reports to Médecins Sans Frontières, the largest organisation operating within the camp.

Aid agencies have largely been absent from the Calais camp, leaving volunteers to fill their place. The UNHCR has a remit to administer care in refugee camps only if a humanitarian crisis has been declared or if invited to do so by the host government. With the clearance of the southern half of the camp, which includes the women and children's centre, under way, the plight of the unaccompanied children has reached crisis point.

Concerns have been raised consistently that a lack of adequate alternative provision for the unaccompanied children - estimated to number up to 500 - has left them at grave risk of falling prey to criminal gangs. In most cases, these children have travelled from their home countries with traffickers.

A spokesperson for Save the Children acknowledged that sexual abuse has been carried out against children in Calais, and called on the British Government to ease the path of entry for children with a legitimate asylum claim.

"We know that unaccompanied children, of whom there are over 400 in the camp and tens of thousands across the continent, are the most vulnerable of the vulnerable. They have travelled hundreds of miles without the protection of adults or families. They face exploitation in all different forms, including sexual exploitation, often at the hands of criminal gangs. Save the Children has seen it in Italy, in

Greece and in Calais too unfortunately. "Many of the children who are in Calais have family in the UK and a right to asylum here but the process is so complex that it can take years. In the meantime they are living in very dangerous situations when they could be safely with their families in the UK."

A spokesperson for Europol said the organisation had declared the figure of 10,000 missing children across the continent to "raise awareness of the vulnerability of unaccompanied minors travelling with the migrant flow".

Médecins Sans Frontières was yesterday unable to confirm having received the reports of sexual abuse against minors. The volunteers with whom The Independent spoke also raised concerns that a sex trade was operating within the camp, saying that boys as young as 13 asked them for condoms. They added that attempts to distribute rape alarms were largely futile as there "is nobody here to hear them".

Oscar Quine

7 March 2016

WARSHIP DISPATCHED TO TURN BACK MIGRANTS

An unprecedented intervention into the migrant crisis in the Aegean Sea will be expanded and joined by a British warship. David Cameron will announce the action today as desperate European leaders meet in Brussels to try to stop another wave of humanity crossing to the EU from Turkey.

A summit today in Brussels - the ninth over the past year - will attempt to address the refugee crisis, with leaders now pinning their hopes on a deal with Turkey to prevent more people from attempting the hazardous journey to Europe. The European Council President, Donald Tusk, who chairs today's summit, toured the main countries on the western Balkans route last week, including Turkey and Greece, as he attempted to pull together a plan to both prevent refugees from leaving Turkey and send them back if they do land in Greece, Italy or other frontline countries.

The Turkish Prime Minister, Ahmet Davutoglu, who will also attend the summit, has promised to take back all non-Syrians who arrive in Greece. However, human rights groups say the EU is shirking its humanitarian responsibilities by using Turkey as its border guard.

"Using Turkey as a 'safe third country' is absurd," said Gauri van Gulik, Amnesty International's deputy director for Europe and Central Asia. "Many refugees still live in terrible conditions, some have been deported back to Syria and security forces have even shot at Syrians trying to cross the border."

The EU has offered Turkey €3bn (£2.3bn) and the prospect of an easy visa regime for Turkish visitors, in return for action to stop the estimated 2.6 million Syrian refugees from leaving Turkish shores. This includes stepping up police and coast guard operations to stop the people smugglers who are still ferrying nearly 2,000 people a day to Greece.

Some of the refugees will be sent back to Turkey by Nato, whose patrols around the Aegean Sea are currently intercepting migrants trying to reach Greece. Those patrols will now be joined by British ships, David Cameron will announce this morning. They will also be expanded into Turkish and Greek territorial waters.

A Royal Navy amphibious landing ship, RFA Mounts Bay, and two border force cutters will join the Nato mission to identify smugglers taking migrants to Greece. "This migration crisis is the greatest challenge facing Europe today," Mr Cameron will say ahead of the summit. "Where we can help, we should. And we've got to break the model of the criminal smugglers and stop the desperate flow of people crammed into makeshift vessels from embarking on a fruitless and perilous journey."

The Nato secretary-general, Jens Stoltenberg, said last night the alliance's mission would use more vessels and deepen co-operation with the EU's Frontex border agency. In February defence ministers ordered the immediate deployment of three Nato vessels to the Aegean Sea. "Now we are going further by actually doing two new things," Mr Stoltenberg told the Associated Press. "We are going into Greek and Turkish territorial waters. We have agreed on arrangements for doing that."

Negotiations with Ankara have been fraught since a deal was first mooted last autumn. At a meeting last November, President Recep Tayyip Erdogan threatened to flood Europe with migrants if EU leaders did not offer him a better deal. But the EU needs Turkey, and is prepared to play up to the increasingly autocratic Mr Erdogan until the deal is fully in place. Indeed, many observers thought it no coincidence that the influential Turkish daily Zaman was closed down by the government last Friday, at a moment when EU leaders were highly unlikely to voice outrage at the silencing of an opposing newspaper.

"The EU is desperate," said Amanda Paul at the European Policy Centre, a Brussels-based think-tank. "This desperation takes the shape of brushing fundamental rights and freedoms under the carpet. Not only does the EU's approach send the message that refugees can be used as leverage, it is also strengthening the increasingly authoritarian and intolerant rule of Erdogan."

Turkey is already home to 2.5 million Syrians and half a million refugees of other nationalities. Under pressure from the EU, it has announced new measures to encourage them to stay rather than looking to start a new life in Europe. Cracking down on the lucrative smuggling industry that operates along the county's Aegean coast may prove a more difficult prospect. Turkey has promised to massively expand its coast guard patrols, but officials say that many migrants and refugees are willing to keep trying to reach Greece until they succeed.

The Turkey deal is only one part of the EU's response to the refugee crisis. Mr Tusk will push the leaders at the summit to close down the Balkan route through which more than one million people have passed since last summer. He also wants the EU to do more to help Greece, whose many islands have been easy landing spots for refugees setting off from Turkey.

Indeed, the Greek coast guard said yesterday that some 400 migrants had been rescued in the Aegean in six separate operations. Turkey's state-run Anadolu news agency said 25 migrants had drowned off the Turkish coast while trying to reach Greece. The Turkish coast guard rescued 15 other migrants off the Aegean Sea resort of Didim.

The Greek Prime Minister, Alexis Tsipras, said he would seek an immediate relocation of migrants stranded on its soil at today's summit and would call for sanctions against EU members that did not "abide by common decisions". But for now, Greece is likely to have to cope on its own with a bottleneck of refugees as its neighbours unilaterally reintroduce border controls.

Leo Cendrowicz

7 March 2016

THE MYTH OF THE HUMANE REFUGEE CAMP

The young mother told me her horror story as we sat drinking tea near the Syrian border. Sadly, it felt all too familiar as she went through her litany of despair: home destroyed, life disrupted, family devastated. Five relatives were killed in the carnage of conflict; she showed me pictures on her phone of one cousin's corpse that was disembowelled in a state prison. "I feel like my head will explode when I remember what life was like before war," she said.

Yet this woman was certain of one thing: she would rather return to Syria despite the savagery on all sides than go back to the refugee camp she fled a few days before we met. It was like prison, she said - echoing words I heard earlier from others. There was no work, no electricity and nothing to do all day, while stores overcharged for food and clothing behind the barbed wire. Her family left their last few possessions to escape. "Here we have nothing but at least we have our freedom."

Her story should be heeded as European and Turkish leaders meet for the latest summit over the migration crisis. As our continent reels in response to refugees such as that woman, along with migrants seeking the sort of life we take for granted, the tone of debate is becoming nastier. And the myths are growing: that Europe is being swamped, that we live in times of unprecedented migration, that walls stop desperate people, that refugees steal jobs, that migrants move for benefits, that evil people smugglers are the primary cause of all the problems.

Europe's panicking politicians are preparing to throw more money at Turkey to persuade it to police its borders better. They want the Turks to restrain 2.75 million Syrians inside their country - which is, incidentally, 137 times the pathetic number Britain plans to accept over five years. One myth in particular needs to be nailed fast: the concept that refugee camps are humane and workable solutions to such crises. Politicians and pundits keep suggesting that we pour cash into these holding pens. Yet as that young mother in Jordan showed, this approach is wrong both morally and practically.

These centres are routinely placed in remote areas by governments to segregate refugees. This is one reason for the failure of the showcase Azraq camp in Jordan, currently holding 32,866 people, although intended for almost 100,000 more. It was designed by the United Nations (and part-funded by Britain) and supposed to reflect the lessons of the past. Yet most Syrians and Iraqis prefer poverty to this dismal outpost in the desert; thousands more risk lethal boats to Europe rather than a supposed place of sanctuary.

Western politicians love going to camps to cuddle children and parade compassion, even as they do their damnedest to stop asylum-seekers arriving anywhere near their own doorsteps. But clearly these institutions do not stop people coming to Europe; the numbers at Zaatari, the biggest camp in Jordan, have also fallen sharply.

Let us focus less on camps in this crisis. They are one more fig leaf for politicians. The key is to let refugees work legitimately, so they can build a fresh start - wherever they are. After all, what human being wants life trapped in limbo? Refugees may have escaped hell, but that does not mean we force them into purgatory.

Ian Birrell

8 March 2016

LIFE ON THE EDGE OF SURVIVAL

Before watching Frontline Doctors: Winter Migrant Crisis (BBC1), I was guilty of boiling down the refugee crisis to a series of headlines and images - overcrowded dinghies sinking in the sea; a dead child on the beach; long queues in the snow; tents in the mud; grey-faced world leaders - but I hadn't put it all together.

Identical twins Chris and Xand van Tulleken did that for viewers very effectively, and the result was an eye-opening hour, mostly as bleak as the leaden grey skies over the camps and checkpoints they visited - but it was an important insight into the very complex situation the world is facing.

The doctor brothers were in Europe to help the medical teams and to show us the migrants behind the headlines. So they were on the beaches of Lesbos; in Athens; in the freezing Balkans; in Berlin; and in Calais and Dunkirk to explain where the people were coming from - Syria, Iraq, and Afghanistan - and where they hoped to go.

The range of ailments they treated were heart-breaking souvenirs from each step of the diverse journeys. There was frostbite from walking for days in freezing temperatures and inadequate footwear; sea urchin spikes in feet from the scrambles to the beach; broken limbs from the altercations with police in the camps; and psychological problems from the sheer hell of it all. They were health issues that any one of us would be unlucky to suffer from, but for the migrants, this was becoming the new normal.

"Thank you for caring," said one, words that made us realise, if we were in any doubt, just how dehumanising it all was.

Only in Germany was there a glimmer of hope. Chris visited the converted Templehof airport, built by the Nazis, now transformed into an efficient shelter. "We are lucky, we get to visit this historical place free," said one good-humoured bloke. As Xand and Chris reconvened in the Kabul Café in the Jungle in Calais, it was only the medical problems the normally upbeat brothers had solutions for.

"I've never felt more lucky in my life," Xand said. I think all viewers would have shared that sentiment.

Sally Newall

8 March 2016

BRITAIN NOT THE LAND OF THEIR DREAMS

The reality faced by young migrant men arriving in the UK, often after arduous journeys of thousands of miles, is that Britain in 2016 is a far cry from the land of their dreams.

A study by experts at the University of Manchester which forms part of a European Commission report on migration has found that the hopes of young migrants arriving here are all too quickly shattered.

While new arrivals want to work hard, start a family, play sport and lead an active social life, many face exclusion and hostility at work, in sports grounds and nightclubs, and also find themselves being unfairly treated by the public and the authorities.

Researchers are now calling for a national effort to help integrate these men into British society so that they no longer feel like second class citizens and can start reaching their full potential for the benefit of the UK economy.

"The majority of the young men we spoke to said they felt fear of victimisation or racism because they feel like second class citizens," said Jon Spencer, from the university's Centre for Criminology and Criminal Justice, who led the study.

"When interviewed, they told us that a lot of their social interactions were awkward and made them feel insecure or had the potential to cause conflict or in some cases violence."

More than one in 10 people in Britain are estimated to be foreign-born, with India, Poland, Pakistan and Ireland traditionally among the biggest sources of new arrivals. The Syrian refugee crisis has focused the public's minds on immigration, with David Cameron announcing this week that Royal Navy warships will join Nato forces intercepting people trying to reach Europe from Turkey.

Immigration is also a key battleground at the heart of the EU referendum, with John Whittingdale, the culture secretary, warning Mr Cameron that he must release the figures showing the "true number" of EU migrants in Britain, amid claims that public services are "creaking at the seams".

Researchers believe that a negative portrayal of migrants by politicians and the media could be making it difficult for those with legitimate rights of residence to settle, with many feeling they are constantly having to justify their status.

The European Commission study involved in-depth interviews with more than 280 migrants aged 16 to 27 in seven countries across Europe, including the UK.

"The young men we interviewed had a right of residence and aren't illegal immigrants, yet society in general isn't making them feel welcome," Mr Spencer said.

"They feel they are constantly having to justify their status and are made to feel like they don't belong here. Many we spoke to told us that they feel as if they are on the wrong side of the law, even if they've done nothing wrong.

"The perception seems to be that these young men are automatically seen at risk of engaging in criminal activity." The researchers say it is vital that national policies are drawn up to help these men to belong and play a part in society and the economy.

"Feeling accepted and part of society is crucial to a young man's sense of wellbeing and can determine the quality of their present and future outlook," Mr Simpson said.

"There needs to be a national effort to help integrate these men and give them a sense of security. If people can feel they are members of society, it builds citizenship.

"It should be driven nationally and delivered locally, with migrant community organisations involved in creating educational strategies and developing language skills.

"These are young men who have an absolute right to be here and want to work, but they don't feel part of society."

"Many of the young men say they are made to feel like criminals, but they have done nothing wrong"

Dean Kirby

9 March 2016

BALKAN ROUTE TO EUROPE SHUT DOWN

Slovenia tightened its borders today as the EU sought to shut down the route used by hundreds of thousands of migrants to reach western Europe.

As Hungary has already put up razorwire fences on its borders, Slovenia's move will force migrants to travel hundreds of miles further north to reach Germany, Sweden or other countries.

Slovenia said only migrants seeking asylum there or with clear humanitarian needs would be allowed in.

Prime Minister Miro Cerar declared the Balkan route used by refugees from Syria and other war zones, as well as by economic migrants, was now effectively "shutting down".

He said the EU was stopping the flow of "irregular migrants" into Europe, which has seen hundreds drown in the Aegean Sea this year and thousands perish in the Mediterranean in 2015.

Serbia announced it would shut its borders with Macedonia and Bulgaria to those without valid documents.

European leaders are seeking a deal with Turkey to take back thousands of migrants crossing into Greece to gain a foothold in the EU. But Ankara wants £4.6 billion in financial support and is demanding the EU accept a genuine refugee for every person returned to Turkey, the speeding-up of accession talks to join the union and the easing of visa restrictions on its citizens.

EU leaders failed to reach an agreement with Turkish Prime Minister Ahmet Davutoglu at a Brussels summit on Monday. But talks are going on with the aim of sealing an agreement at an EU summit next week.

The UN and human rights groups have warned that the migrant "return" policy may be illegal.

Four British ships are being deployed as part of a Nato mission to boost intelligence-gathering about human trafficking gangs taking migrants from Turkey to Greece.

The migrant crisis has split the EU and even cast into doubt the future of its passport-free Schengen zone.

Eight countries have tightened border controls, leaving thousands of migrants stranded in Greece. David Cameron has refused to offer a safe haven to any of the migrants who have already arrived in the EU.

Britain will instead accept at least 20,000 over five years from refugee camps in the Syria region.

Nicholas Cecil

9 March 2016

IS THE EU READY TO USE FORCE?

The mood came perilously close to euphoria. The deal reached in Brussels after eight hours of talks offered the first hope for six months that the EU might have a workable plan for addressing the human emergency unfolding on and around its shores. Chancellor Angela Merkel, it seemed, had worked another miracle. The EU Commission President, Jean-Claude Juncker, spoke of a "game changer".

Re-examined in the cold light of day, however, the outline agreement raises a host of questions, of principle and practice. Let's start with the practice.

The central idea is that all "irregular migrants", including Syrians, who arrive on Greek territory from Turkey will be sent back. For every one person returned to Turkey, a Syrian refugee who is recognised as such in Turkey will be resettled in the EU. It is an ingenious scheme, designed to destroy the business model of peopletraffickers and break the link - as David Cameron has put it - between boarding a boat and reaching the EU. Those returned to Turkey will be sent to the back of the resettlement queue.

But just imagine the scenes. Even apprehending, let alone returning, wouldbe asylum-seekers will be far easier said than done. The Greek, Turkish and Italian shores are a smuggler's paradise. Nato ships may be helping with surveillance, but the numbers needed to screen those arriving will be large, and neither Greece nor Italy has taken kindly to the notion of EU officials policing their sovereign borders.

How is it proposed that hundreds of people, including fit young men, pregnant women and small children, will be embarked on to ships destined for somewhere they desperately do not want to go? Remember those Central European stations last year? Once, force might have been used out of media sight. But mobile phones have changed all that - as has the vigilance of those who doughtily champion the refugees' cause.

As the Calais Jungle illustrates, many would rather take the chance of a safer, or better, life in the UK tomorrow than more orderly and sanitary living conditions in France today.

For all these reasons it is hard to see how the agreement with Turkey, as currently couched, can work without at least the show (if not the use) of force. Are the EU governments prepared for this? Are they braced for the inevitable outcry? Is Germany? Is Sweden? More to the point, is such coercion what the European Union is about? The thinking behind the deal must be that, after some people have been demonstratively returned, and equivalent numbers of Syrians have been flown to an EU country - to much media fanfare and warm local receptions - the message will get through, and the market for traffickers will decline. If Merkel's words of welcome girdled the Earth with such speed last year, perhaps the opposite message can do the same. Hope, though, has an admirable habit of trumping despair, and while there is little purpose in reprising the past, the truth needs to be acknowledged. The proposed new arrangements amount to little more than a belated attempt by the EU to regain control of its own borders.

The refugee crisis is widely seen as a failure of the Schengen agreement. But Schengen, which abolished frontier controls between its signatories, did not fail. What failed was control of the EU's external border on which the viability of Schengen was predicated. If the external border can be secured, the new internal controls - those fences and border posts - can be dismantled again, as Merkel, for one, so fervently wishes.

Reasserting the external border, however, also means strengthening what has often been criticised, including by human rights champions inside the EU, as "fortress Europe". Their complaint is that almost no one has been able to enter the EU legally, so even those qualified for asylum must in one way or another circumvent the law. The scheme to resettle Syrians from Turkish camps helps to address this dilemma - but only for Syrians, and only from Turkey.

This is also where principle comes in. If people arrive, albeit having paid traffickers, with a legitimate claim to asylum can the EU (or Greece, or Italy) legally turn them back? The answer from EU officials in the early hours of yesterday was yes, because they had voluntarily left a place of safety. But the argument will surely be open to challenge, both because it would deny all refugees any choice in their destination and because of the political situation in Turkey.

There is a further point relating to Nato.

If its assistance is required, in whatever form, to secure the EU's borders, does this not undermine a distinction that the EU has always insisted upon: between the political and economic Union, and the quite separate military alliance? It is a blurring of lines that Russia, among others, would gleefully seize upon as proof that it was right all along about the EU and Ukraine.

In the end, all these qualms could turn out to be academic. The deal done this week has bought Angela Merkel time - the details will be hammered out only in 10 days' time, after crucial regional elections in Germany. Thereafter, the price demanded by Turkey could well be rejected as too high. It includes not only more money for refugee facilities, but visa-free travel for Turks to the Schengen zone, to start as early as June. France could join the "new" EU member states in baulking at this, while David Cameron, too, might object to any visa liberalisation in the run-up to the referendum - even though it would affect only Schengen countries, of which the UK is not one.

Even if terms can be agreed, those Syrian refugees who would be resettled from Turkey will need somewhere to go. Which takes us back to the failed EU quotas of last summer. The quest of the refugees for safety; the hopes of so many others for a better life, and the earnings of the traffickers all have a long way left to run.

Mary Dejevsky

12 March 2016

TEUTONIC DONALD TRUMP

His campaign speeches have been compared by some to the wartime propaganda of Joseph Goebbels, yet the new bogeyman on Germany's xenophobic right seems not to give a damn. When Björn Höcke talks about "1,000 years of Germany" and the threat posed by migrants to the "Fatherland" and the "German Volk [people]", his supporters go wild with enthusiasm.

Mr Höcke, 43, an ex-schoolteacher who was raised in the former West Germany, is the most popular and radical politician in Germany's recently formed Alternative for Germany (AfD). The vehemently anti-immigration party is set to make sweeping gains in this weekend's socalled "Super Sunday" elections in three states because of its outright opposition to Chancellor Angela Merkel's refugee policies, which meant the country registered nearly 1.1 million people as asylumseekers last year.

Mr Höcke, the AfD leader in Thuringia, in eastern Germany, draws crowds of up to 8,000 to his rallies. He takes delight in breaking with Germany's "politically correct" post-war consensus which still holds that anything that hints even vaguely of the Third Reich is out. His liberal detractors are appalled.

Die Welt newspaper recently commented: "For decades success in German politics for a man like Björn Höcke seemed impossible. In the meantime, the seemingly impossible has become possible".

In a rainy, windswept market square in the down-at-heel town of Raguhn in eastern Saxony-Anhalt earlier this week, Mr Höcke was doing his best to sustain his reputation as a Teutonic Donald Trump as he campaigned ahead of Super Sunday.

"We are the tortured German Volk!" he bellowed at hundreds of his supporters from the back of a truck. "I am no longer prepared to accept the policies of Merkel. They are ruining Germany.

This Chancellor - she must go - we need a patriot in the Chancellery," he added to loud applause. A "Refugees welcome" sign showing a queue of migrants entering Ms Merkel's office waved above heads in the crowd.

Tomorrow's state elections in Saxony-Anhalt, Baden Württemberg and Rhineland-Palatinate are set to be a referendum on Ms Merkel's policies and a bellwether for next year's general election. Before the recent EU-Turkey summit on the migration crisis, opinion polls showed that 81 percent of Germans believed that Ms Merkel had lost control of the refugee crisis.

In Saxony-Anhalt, the AfD is expected to win up to 20 percent of the vote and become the third most powerful political party in the state after Ms Merkel's Christian Democrats and the reform communist Die Linke ("The Left") party. In the two other west German states, the Af D is also on course to notch up doubledigit percentage. While other parties have said they will not share power with the AfD, its performance could complicate efforts to form coalition governments. Big gains in this weekend's elections are also likely to mean that the AfD will end up with parliamentary seats in eight of Germany's 16 federal states and have a serious chance of entering the national parliament in Berlin in 2017.

The AfD advocates the return to a "Europe of Fatherlands" and the expulsion of criminal asylum-seekers. Last month, the party's leader, Frauke Petry, suggested that border guards should be empowered to shoot illegal immigrants. The 40-year-old businesswoman later claimed that her remarks had been taken out of context.

In Raguhn, Hannes Loth, a local AfD politician, attempted to downplay claims that his party was xenophobic. He insisted that its chief concern was to expel rejected asylum-seekers who were taking up scarce hostel space that could accommodate genuine Syrian war refugees. "The Merkel government won't kick them out," he told The Independent, adding: "I admire your David Cameron. He leads the way on how to deal with welfare scrounging in Europe."

The party started out in 2013 with a Eurosceptic agenda opposing the single currency. But in an internal putsch in July last year, an initially moderate leadership under economics professor Bernd Lucke was ousted. Ms Petry and other vociferous anti-immigration politicians took the helm.

The AfD's agenda is not just about migration. Its policies aim to make Germany a "Fatherland once again". It wants schools to bring back 19th-century "Prussian values" of order and discipline, and laws that will oblige museums and theatres to strengthen "identification with one's own country".

Germany's political pundits are divided on whether the AfD will remain a serious political force. Manfred Güllner of the Forsa public polling group argues that the party has already reached its zenith and that its popularity will wane as soon as the refugee crisis eases. But Werner Patzelt, a political scientist at Dresden University of Technology, thinks that the polls this weekend may be the beginning of a major shake-up. He believes the AfD could even end up sharing power with Ms Merkel's conservatives in Berlin. "A horrific scenario threatens us," he said.

Mr Höcke is not angling for the job of Chancellor just yet: "I am a long-distance runner, not a sprinter. I don't have to put myself in the top position immediately," he has insisted.

Tony Paterson

26 March 2016

JIHADISTS NIGHTMARE

Western security agencies are blind to the terror plots being hatched in the Middle East because of the unknown number of jihadists who have been dispatched to Europe by Islamic State and al-Qaeda.

This worrying gap in intelligence was cruelly exposed in Tuesday's bomb attacks in Brussels and reinforced by the arrests of a dozen more terror suspects trained in Syria who have been picked up in security operations across Belgium and France. While many were known to the Belgian and French agencies as petty criminals, the crucial intelligence about their travel to and from Syria was not.

The blame for this intelligence failure has been placed on the growing number of migrants fleeing the Middle East for Europe and terrorists disguising themselves as refugees. But the refugee crisis is merely a political diversion.

Since the start of the Syrian conflict five years ago tens of thousands of Islamist extremists and jihadists have left Europe to join terrorist groups in the region and a half of them have returned home to Europe. If anything the more recent migration crisis has increased levels of security and led to the tightening of border controls, making it more difficult to travel unhindered across Europe. And a terrorist with an EU passport can always find much safer and less unpleasant means travelling between states.

It was only in 2013 that Western governments woke up to the dangers of young Muslims travelling to Syria, being trained as terrorists and sent back to Europe to act out the kind of atrocities that were witnessed in Paris and Brussels. MI5 describes this as the "terrorism blowback" - fighters returning to the UK intent on carrying out bombings and shootings. One Whitehall security source said: "All we can know is that they have been in a war zone and come into contact with any number of bad people.

"Now they are back in Britain after they have done their jihad but how many put the whole experience behind them and get on with whatever they were doing before they left? And how many are planning terrorism?" The security services estimate that 800 British jihadists have gone to Syria, others put the number as high as 2,000. I have been told of two British citizens who joined Islamic State and returned to the UK without any contact with UK security services. One of them made the trip three times without any questions raised before dying in a suicide attack in Iraq two years ago. The other didn't like IS and so came home. There must be many more who have made similar trips outside the sight of security services.

Even when suspects are known to MI5 and the Metropolitan Police there are simply not enough resources to subject them all to 24/7 surveillance. Besides, close security doesn't always work. At least two terror suspects have managed to flee the UK for Syria while under tight surveillance from the security services.

"If you live in a democratic country then it is very hard to stop people leaving the UK," a security source said.

The human blunders of the French, Belgian and German intelligence agencies in recent months demonstrate that missed intelligence opportunities can cost lives.

Turkey's unheeded warning to Belgium and Holland about one of the Brussels bombers shows how difficult it is to get national agencies to work together. This week the former head of MI6, Sir Richard Dearlove, delivered a withering attack on some of the intelligence sharing agencies across Europe. "Though the UK participates in various European and Brusselsbased security bodies, they are of little consequence," he said. "The Club de Berne, made up of European Security Services; the Club de Madrid, made up of European Intelligence Services; Europol and the Situation Centre in the European Commission are, generally speaking, little more than forums for the exchange of analysis and views."

Here in the UK, MI5 and the Met's Counter Terrorism Command have foiled seven plots linked to Syria in the past year. But the unknown number of violent jihadists living in British communities means they cannot be expected to win every time.

Robert Verkaik

26 March 2016

HOPE TURNS TO DESPAIR

Even before it became a holding pen, Moria was a pretty poor registration centre, unable to provide basic facilities and painfully slow to process the thousands of refugees and migrants who arrive on the shores of Lesbos every week.

But since midnight on Sunday, when the new EU-Turkey migrant deal came into force, refugees have been picked up by the coastguard and transported directly to Moria by the Greek authorities.

The camp has become an open-air prison, a compound of temporary buildings on a hill overlooking the coast of this island, not far from Turkey's Mediterranean coast. It is to here that all arrivals must wait for the news their long struggle to reach Europe will almost certainly get them no further than the Greek islands.

They will be returned to Turkey, which the European Union has now declared a safe country, in its bid to stem the biggest refugee crisis since the Second World War.

The lightning fast implementation of the deal, signed last Friday, has stretched to the limit the capacity of the Greek government, which has no means to process the asylum claims that everyone who arrives has the right to make. Those who came looking for peace and a better life have instead found themselves locked up, and handed detention papers. In response, aid agencies have dropped out of their involvement at the centre one by one, refusing to be associated with the

detention of migrants - among whom are more than 100 unaccompanied children. Oxfam this week said the development was "an offence"
to Europe's values.

"They have told us nothing," says Naima Abdullah, 28, speaking
through the chain link fence, her four-year-old daughter Mirna by her
side. She paid $2,000 for herself, Mirna, and her one-month-old baby
to cross the sea from Turkey after fleeing air strikes in rural Damascus
three months ago. She arrived on Sunday (20 March), in the first boats
after the deal came into force. But four days later, she still hadn't been
given an opportunity to register a claim for asylum.

And as the numbers grow, observers worry the only possible outcome will be the mass expulsions Europe has promised to avoid.
Nadine Abuasil, 25, said she came to Lesbos because life in Turkey
since she fled Deraa in Syria a month ago was not worth living. Her
family were blackmailed for money by local gangs, and there was no
work in a country that is expensive to live in. "We cannot go back to
Turkey," she says simply. She and her 23-year-old brother arrived on
Sunday after a five hour boat journey during which two men died.
They had apparently suffocated.

She points to the ground of the detention centre. "We would rather die here than in Turkey." Her brother, Mohammed, was no less
emphatic when asked what he'd do if he was forced to return. "I don't
speak English," he says. "But: kill myself, kill myself."

The deal has been decried by human rights groups and legal experts who question if Turkey can be considered a safe third country
for the forcible return of migrants, and if Greece, which has floun-
dered under the pressure of more than one million refugees arrivals
in the past year, is capable of processing asylum claims - even with
promised outside help.

"Greece has effectively been asked to build an asylum system in
two weeks," says Camino Mortera, a research fellow for the Centre for
European Reform and a specialist in EU law. "The EU claims there
won't be returns en masse but if you are not able to process people in
a regulated fashion, how else are they going to deal with this?" As a
detention centre Moria is barely adequate, including to the task of
holding people in - a handful jump the fence at ease and unnoticed,
disappearing into the woodland. They have nowhere to go once
they're out and often come back. People have been forced to sleep on
the chalky gravel, wrapped in blankets. Among them are a frail elderly

man, and Elham, 14, from Afghanistan who fled along with her family from threats from the Taliban.

"We asked the police for information, they just say 'We don't know'," said Elham. Tensions are simmering, with accusations some nationalities are receiving preferential treatment over others.

Naima Abdullah, with her two small children, wants to reach Germany, where her husband is now claiming asylum. It's not clear what will happen to the many families that have been separated this way. Much about the deal is unclear, even to the Greek authorities. "It's not clear how long people will stay," said UNHCR spokesperson Boris Cheshirkov . "It's still not clear how the deal will be implemented, how Greece will be given capability to deal with asylum claims."

Tove Ernst, a spokesperson for migration at the European Commission said the intention was to have people moved from the facilities swiftly, adding: "Detention in cases of returns should always be limited."

Frontex border agency this week called on EU member states to step up and provide extra personnel to help authorities on Lesbos manage the new deal. So far, only 396 of 1,500 requested police officers have been offered. There are plans to send an extra 50 immigration experts, with five arriving from Turkey this week.

Marios Andriotis, a senior adviser to the Lesbos mayor, is visibly strained. He said the local government was doing its best to provide for new arrivals. But, he added: "We are a small municipality and we do not decide the union's policies. We are looking for a contingency plan, a waiting area where we could accommodate 5,000 to 10,000 people." The deal's success relies on people like Ms Abdullah deciding to wait their turn under the one-for-one scheme, under which Europe has agreed to take a Syrian refugee directly from Turkey, in exchange for each Syrian Turkey accepts back from Greece.

The numbers have shown some signs of slowing. Coast guards heading out for a patrol on Thursday said they didn't expect to pick up anyone.

Fadi, 23, who declined to give his family name, arrived in Lesbos after fleeing army conscription in Syria. He escaped to Turkey at the end of last year, paying bribes along the way to the regime and to Isis. When he left Turkey, he had no idea an effective prison would be awaiting him in Greece.

He says he wouldn't have come if he had known. "They treat us like animals here," he said, shouting across a ditch that runs along one side of Moria's chainlink fence. "I feel like I am in Syria." Still, he doesn't think the deal will contain the refugees for long. "People are fleeing a war. They will find a way," he said. In any case, Europe agreed to take only 72,000 Syrians under the plan; more than twice that number arrived in Greece last October alone. And there is doubt that member states will hold up their end of the bargain in taking in refugees; previous attempts to impose a quota system to share the burden have swiftly fallen apart. Europe hopes, too, many can be persuaded to stay in Turkey. It has promised an extra €3bn to Ankara to help provide aid to its 2.7 million Syrian refugees. But with little work and education for Syrians in Turkey, many are on the point of destitution and may take some convincing that they have a future there.

If people come anyway, the Greek islands will be swiftly overwhelmed. Their combined facilities have a capacity of just 7,490, already more than half full. And in the first five days since the deal came into effect, more than 1,400 had made the journey to the islands.

In the midst of all this, as ever, are those who hoped to arrive to a Europe that would welcome them with open walls, even if not with open arms. "I want to tell Europe: I do not want to go to Turkey. I want to see my husband in Germany," said Ms Abuasil. "Syria is awful. If it was not awful, we would not have left."

Emma Gatten

EPILOGUE

AVOIDING AN APOCALYPSE

4 April 2016

AN ENDURING AND ENDEMIC MIGRANT CRISIS

With the recapture of Palmyra last week and the assault on al-Qaryatain, 60 miles to the west, this weekend, Syrian government forces backed by Russian air power and artillery seem poised to dislodge Islamic State (IS) from the populated western part of Syria. IS is bracing itself for an all-out onslaught to expel it from its spiritual and operational capital, Raqqa.

The advance of the Russian-Assad forces alliance is a game-changer in the Syrian crisis. It makes it harder to demand the removal of Assad in the UN-sponsored peace talks in Geneva.

While the rout of IS has established a new reality on the ground, the wider aspects of the crisis — in particular the turmoil caused by the huge number of Syrian refugees and the wider spread of IS into empire-building in Africa and terror in Europe — are far from resolved.

The loose alliance of Western nations led by the US and regional powers is struggling to keep up. The allies seem now to lack the practical means, strategy and policies — and even at times the real will — to rise to the challenge.

The new fact on the ground is that Russian efforts since autumn last year have ensured that the Assad forces have their own enclave in the western parts of Syria. Russia has guaranteed its toehold on the eastern Mediterranean at the bases of Tartus and Latakia.

It is open to doubt, however, if the Assad regime could ever again rule the whole of Syria. Given the brutal methods used by its forces — targeting civilians with barrel bombs, cluster munitions and the like — few among the Sunni population will accept the Alawitedominated junta again. This means that many of the five or six million refugees who have already fled will not return.

This is producing intolerable strains on neighbouring countries Lebanon, Jordan and Turkey, which now hosts more than three million refugees. Turkey is still very much the awkward ally. It is vital for stemming the flow of refugees from the eastern Mediterranean, yet its war aims in Syria set it apart.

Turkey sees Assad and the Syrian Kurds as enemies — though the latter have been supported by the Americans, especially in the defeat of IS forces in Kobane. It regards them as allies of the Kurdish Workers Party, the PKK, locked into an insurgency in south-east Turkey for decades. Though IS has been blamed for terror attacks in Turkey lately, the Erdogan regime seems to rank it behind Assad's forces and the PKK in the hierarchy of Turkey's enemies.

Turkey and Greece are from today supposed to be implementing the complicated swap arrangement designed by the EU and its allies to stem the flow of refugees across the Aegean. Refugees arriving on Greek shores illegally are to be turned around and dumped back in camps on the Turkey-Syria border. In turn a similar number of registered refugees will be admitted to Europe from camps inside Turkey.

Neither Greece nor Turkey is prepared for this elaborate choreography, which smacks of crude and short-term expediency by the EU, including the British. In a 21st-century version of Ethelred the Unready's Danegeld, billions of euros have been thrown at the Turks, hoping that, like the Vikings, the refugees and their problems will go away.

Even if a ceasefire is achieved in Syria this summer, the issue of IS remains. It controls a large part of Iraq and parts of eastern and southern Syria. From Afghanistan to the Mediterranean it is claiming new governorates. The latest of these are at Sirte in Libya and Kunar Province in Afghanistan, where it has lined up with the Haqqani insurgents and the Pakistan Taliban.

The terrorist attacks in Paris and now in Brussels have shown the IS terror operation to be wider, and perhaps deeper, than hitherto understood.

Both the IS enclave in Libya and the discoveries in Brussels reveal the movement's ability to adapt and innovate rapidly. Across Libya, IS is moving into human trafficking as well as commerce in fuel and food to Tunisia. Beyond Tunisia, Algeria and Morocco are targets, with Morocco being the new jumping-off point for Syrian and Iraqi refugees paying to get into Europe via the Spanish enclaves of Ceuta and Melilla — slivers of EU territory on the African continent.

Italy and Britain are leading discussions about sending in a small peacekeeping force to protect a new coalition administration in Tripoli to try to bring stability to Libya. Britain would offer 1,000 service personnel but not in a combat role. Thus David Cameron can't be accused of putting "boots on the ground". This makes the proposal appear the empty gesture that it is.

IS fully understands the failure to commit. In part Britain's problem is that it doesn't even have the forces now that it had for the shortsighted international mission four years ago which got rid of Colonel Gaddafi but contributed hugely to the anarchy in which IS now thrives.

In his recent interview with the Standard the Australian strategist David Kilcullen said that much of Western strategic and political thinking is focused on the recent past rather than what is new in the present. "Sometimes what would have worked 24 hours ago won't work at all today," he said.

In handling refugees and facing the changes of IS's terror strategy we have witnessed the collective inadequacy of multinational bodies, particularly Nato and the EU. Across Europe there is increasingly little confidence in the EU. It is seen as failing the test on refugees and terror — though leaving Europe may make things worse on these fronts for the UK.

The problem is to address the tripleheaded challenges of Syria-Iraq, refugees and IS in terms of today, not the past. The refugee and migrant crisis is set to be as bad or worse than last year, and it will be different.

The migrant issue is enduring and endemic: it is part of the process of humanity doubling in number in just over a century, and in conditions of increasing environmental and climatic stress. Europe has to operate collectively for its security and stability, otherwise it won't exist for much longer. We need a radical change in thinking, planning and the will to act. Otherwise last year's disasters could become next year's catastrophe.

Robert Fox

PHOTO CAPTIONS AND COPYRIGHTS

ALSO AVAILABLE FROM THE INDEPENDENT

CPSIA information can be obtained
at www.ICGtesting.com
Printed in the USA
LVOW04s1330170816
500767LV00032B/728/P